WALES

of one hundred years ago

Motor car and passengers, possibly by Isaac Haley of Glanbrân mansion

WALES

of one hundred years ago

R. IESTYN HUGHES &
PAUL O'LEARY

LLYFRGELL GENEDLAETHOL CYMRU
THE NATIONAL LIBRARY OF WALES
SUTTON PUBLISHING

First published in the United Kingdom in 1999 by
Sutton Publishing Limited · Phoenix Mill
Thrupp · Stroud · Gloucestershire · GL5 2BU

British Library Cataloguing in Publication Data
A catalogue record for this book is available from the British Library

ISBN 0 7509 1713 X

Half-title photograph: Conwy. John Thomas
Title page photograph: Child on donkey at Aberystwyth. Arthur Lewis
Endpapers, front: Deunant school, girls class, 1904. J.G. Davies; back: Deunant school, boys class, 1904. J.G. Davies

™ ALAN SUTTON™ and SUTTON™ are the
trade marks of Sutton Publishing Limited

Typeset in 11/13 pt Bembo
Typesetting and origination by Sutton Publishing Limited.
Printed in Great Britain by WBC Ltd, Bridgend.

Fisher children, Tenby by Francis Frith & Co.

CONTENTS

Playing at gypsy life. D.C. Harries

Wales depicted as Owen Glyndûr, printed by Vincent Brooks, Day & Son, London

A TIME OF CHANGE

In his *Gossiping Guide to Wales*, published in 1904, Ashew Roberts warned prospective visitors against succumbing to hackneyed stereotypes about the country and its inhabitants. Instead, he advised them to observe without prejudice the people they encountered:

some visitors come to Wales with preconceived ideas, and naturally try to fit all they see with their previous notions. Others cross the borders in utter ignorance of what they are going to see . . . and make Welshmen answer in English all the questions they ask, and fall foul of the nation and natives, as dirty and dreary, stupid and vindictive, barren and wholly unprofitable; and their recollections of the Principality are something like those of a grimly facetious gentleman who remarked, after a fortnight's tour in horribly wet weather, that he 'went into Wales expecting to find mountains, but met only ills'.

A cursory look at the photographic and written record of the years around the turn of the century reinforces the value of Roberts's advice, for even though the Welsh were among the smaller nations of Europe there was no single Wales to conform to a visitor's expectations. By this date Wales was a country of variety and stark contrasts, comprising a patchwork of differing ways of life, two major language communities and a plethora of old and new customs jostling in competition with one another.

The decades either side of the turn of the century witnessed an increasing confidence in Welsh nationality. New institutions such as the Welsh Rugby Union (1881), the federal University of Wales, composed of colleges at Aberystwyth, Bangor and Cardiff (1893), and a National Museum and National Library were created. That this national consciousness was a development of recent vintage can be gauged by the dismissive entry in *Encyclopaedia*

The brake 'Blodwen' taking passengers to see the sights around the Aberystwyth area. Arthur Lewis

Britannica in the 1860s – 'For Wales, see England' – while as late as the 1880s Bishop Basil Hughes of St David's could speak of Wales as no more than 'a geographical expression'. National confidence in cultural matters was not matched by a determination to establish a political identity for the country, and those who dreamed of emulating Ireland's drive for Home Rule were to be disappointed.

Cultural confidence was securely rooted in economic expansion. Everywhere society was in the throes of swift, and frequently disorienting, change. The centre of gravity of Welsh society shifted further to the south as the pell-mell growth of the coal industry created new towns and villages in the narrow valleys of the coalfield where previously there had been only a scattered and sparse rural population. As the pits multiplied they sucked in migrants from other parts of Wales and beyond to work in the hazardous and unfamiliar world below ground. Because the industry was export-oriented the ports of the south Wales coast also grew in size and stature as the ships carrying Welsh coal to destinations around the globe grew in number. New docks and even an entirely new port (at Barry) were signs of unrestrained expansion and a faith in the future. By contrast, the slate-quarrying communities of the north-west grew more slowly and developed on a much smaller scale. Unlike most of the coalmining settlements of the south, the slate communities drew their workforce exclusively from adjacent areas and so remained entirely Welsh-speaking.

In the countryside, the tide was finally turning against the centuries-long domination of the landlords. They had been weakened by political reform and soon many would begin to sell parcels of their land, much of which was purchased by the tenants who sought their freedom in the ownership of the land they tilled. However, the real losers in rural Wales were the farm labourers who increasingly faced the unpalatable choice of enduring a pitifully low standard of living at home or venturing elsewhere in search of work.

One of the burning questions of the day was the changing role and status of women in society. As the new secondary schools and the colleges of the University of Wales opened their doors to girls, small numbers of women began to enter higher education. Some found avenues out of traditional domestic roles by qualifying as schoolteachers. But, in spite of increasing access to education, the majority of women remained untouched by these developments. In agricultural areas women's labour remained essential to successful farming, while in the ports some women found employment labouring at the docks. However, because the economic life of most parts of Wales was dominated by heavy industry, work opportunities for women outside the home were scarce. Consequently, for most women the home remained the centre of their activities. In addition to child-minding, housework in the pit areas involved the endless tasks of cooking and cleaning, as well as the back-breaking daily chore of preparing baths from water heated on the open fire for dust-black miners. Such laborious tasks made the life of the miner's wife an endless drudge.

Social change had important implications for the vitality of the Welsh language, for by 1901 only a little over half the

Barry dock in 1899. Francis Frith & Co.

Welsh lady. John Thomas

population of Wales was able to speak the indigenous tongue. This was a development of momentous proportions, because during the first decade of the twentieth century Welsh-speakers ceased to be a majority in their own land for the first time in history. One of the notable developments of these years was the increase in bilingualism as the English language slowly gained ground. For the remainder of the century strenuous attempts would be made to arrest the precipitous decline in the number of native speakers and to strengthen the position of the language among the young. Nevertheless, the picture was not unremittingly bleak before 1914. Because the indigenous population was growing so rapidly there were more speakers of Welsh at the dawn of the new century than ever before – as many as a million if the thriving expatriate Welsh-speaking communities in English cities like Liverpool, Manchester and London and those in the United States are included.

Inevitably, rapid change gave rise to deep-seated social tensions. The unquestioned faith in unending progress and ever-greater achievements which characterised Victorian and Edwardian Wales received a set back in the decade before the First World War. In these years a view gained ground that the bonds holding society together were dissolving as unrest spread. The South Wales Miners' Federation was born out of the bitter strike of 1898 which brought an end to decades of peaceful collaboration between employers and men. Until this date trade unions had sought to defend the interests of the miners without upsetting the balance of power between employer and employee. The miners' leader William Abraham (1842–1922), known more widely by his bardic name of 'Mabon', was the epitome of class collaboration, always preferring to trim his sails to avoid conflict rather than confronting the coalowners head-on. His deep-seated belief that half a loaf was better than none at all determined the

Rheidol Foundry apprentices.
Arthur Lewis

tenor of industrial relations for decades. Mabon exerted a moderating influence on the miners, but that influence gradually waned in the face of the growth of socialism and the emergence of a more militant generation of leaders.

'The Fed', as the Miners' Federation was known colloquially, can justifiably lay claim to be the most influential institution in Welsh life during the first half of the twentieth century. It shaped the political outlook of many of the country's foremost political leaders, like Aneurin Bevan (1897–1960), providing them with the education necessary for representing their people in industry and Parliament. Neither was slate quarrying immune from unrest: the longest strike in British – and possibly European – history at that time occurred in the slate-quarrying settlements of the north-west between 1900 and 1903 as the rapacious Lord Penrhyn attempted to crush his workers' independence.

But it was the so-called 'Great Unrest' of 1910–12 which established the reputation of south Wales as a hotbed of discontent and left-wing political agitation. Troops were deployed extensively in the region, controversially authorised by Winston Churchill as Home Secretary in the Liberal government; a reputation for callousness in his treatment of ordinary workers would dog him for the remainder of his political career, not even being fully extinguished by his role as the country's leader in the Second World War. The Tonypandy riots of 1910 have acquired a special notoriety, but even worse events occurred elsewhere. At Llanelli during the railway workers' strike in 1911 two people were shot by troops. That same year anti-Chinese disturbances erupted at Cardiff as well as anti-Jewish riots at Tredegar in Monmouthshire. Social discontent bubbled below the surface

in many towns and villages, erupting into numerous strikes and disturbances.

In fact, there is a sharp contrast between the splendour of the investiture of Prince Edward as Prince of Wales at Caernarfon Castle in 1911 and the tense atmosphere which permeated industrial south Wales at the same time. At Caernarfon, David Lloyd George basked in the reflected glory of the sumptuous costumes and well-rehearsed ceremonial of a newly minted royal pageant in front of cheering and adulatory crowds, as troops in their ceremonial livery accompanied the Prince to the castle; meanwhile in the southern coalfield, troops were billeted in readiness to deal with unruly strikers. Large numbers of infantry and cavalry were stationed for use against the civilian population, and there were several skirmishes with the workers. There could be no sharper contrast between the two different faces which Wales presented to the world. Revolutionary ideas about workers' control were disseminated in the coalmining valleys and the Rhondda achieved an enduring reputation as a simmering cauldron of unrest. The village of Tonypandy achieved fame not only as the site of a riot, but also as the place which produced a famous document espousing the belief that the workers should take ownership of the industry in which they worked. In some ways, *The Miners' Next Step* (1912) represents the high point of that intense dissatisfaction with the arrangement of society which characterised those unsettled pre-war years, yet its clarion call to revolutionary action was ignored by the majority. There is no clearer indication of this than the enthusiastic response to the call to arms when war broke out in 1914, a phenomenon which was as pronounced a feature of life in Wales as it was elsewhere.

Chapter 1

WALES IN CAMERA

It is generally accepted that, after a long period of gestation, 1839 is the 'birth date' of photography. This was the year that Louis Jacques Mandé Daguerre released to the world details of his daguerreotype process. Using a simple camera and lens, he was able to capture a hidden or 'latent' image onto a silver coated metal plate.

In England, at the time the daguerreotype was unveiled, William Henry Fox Talbot was working on his own photographic invention, the calotype process. The calotype uses a coated paper to capture the scene and when developed and fixed provides a negative image from which many positive copies can be produced. The image is rather indistinct in comparison with the fine detail found in the daguerreotype, but it is this negative/positive process which is the foundation upon which modern photography has been built.

Wales made its own contribution to the early development and practice of photography. Welsh men and women were among the earliest pioneers of the medium as it emerged from the realms of scientific experiment to become a practical application. One of the most notable of these early practitioners was a Swansea clergyman, the Revd Calvert Richard Jones. He was friendly with John Dillwyn Llewelyn, the pivotal figure in a group of early photographers known as the 'Swansea Circle', and with William Henry Fox Talbot himself. Llewelyn's daughter, Thereza Mary Dillwyn Llewelyn was also a fine photographer, and one of the earliest women practitioners. The early photographers mostly saw their practice as the application of science to the artful rendition of nature, rather than as a saleable craft.

Up to the mid-1850s, the practice of photography was confined to a very select few professionals and well-to-do amateurs. This situation was to change radically when, in 1851, a technological development made photography a cheaper and more practical proposition. It was in that year that Frederick Scott Archer announced a new photographic process that he did not attempt to

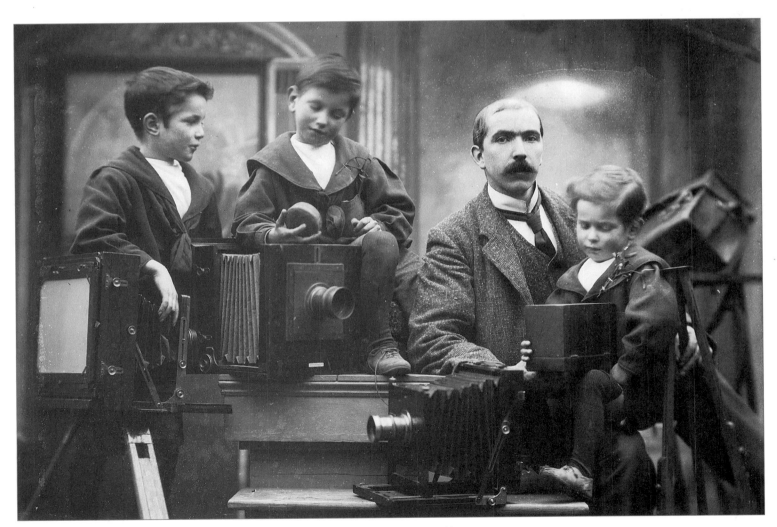

D.C. Harries and family. Self-portrait

Dick Pugh, joiner. John Thomas

patent and that could therefore be used freely without practitioners having to pay any licence fees. The wet collodion process promised and delivered much. It irresistibly combined the best elements of both the daguerreotype and calotype by providing a highly detailed image which, based on a negative/positive process, could be copied innumerable times. It succeeded in combining these virtues by utilising a glass plate negative coated with a light sensitive 'collodion' mixture.

Studios sprang up all around the country as a new breed of photographer, intent on making a decent living, took up the baton. Very often these photographers, enticed by the hope of rich pickings, learnt their craft 'on the job'. The wet collodion process demanded long exposure times – often of several minutes – and the resultant images, though capable of being of very high technical quality, were often necessarily contrived in terms of composition. The cameras were very bulky and the processing of the plates and the printing rather tricky. This discouraged the majority from taking outdoor scenes, or documenting their sitters in their natural context, though an important minority did accomplish this with stunning results.

It was the development of the carte-de-visite from the late 1850s which helped make photography truly popular. By means of a multiple lens camera and other technological advances it was possible to record many small images on a single negative plate. These would be printed, cut and stuck onto a 4 in by 2 in card, thereby creating a classic 'calling card'. Photographers would sell carte portraits of notables and by the 1860s the Victorian public collected them avidly. Another format, that of the larger cabinet card, also became popular and for many years was synonymous with photographic portraiture.

Taking tea. D.C. Harries

It was during this era of frantic development and expansion that John Thomas of Cellan in Cardiganshire started his own photographic business, the 'Cambrian Gallery', in Liverpool, sometimes jokingly called 'the capital of north Wales' due to the large number of expatriates living and working there. Having once earned his living as a travelling salesman of cartes-de-visite he was aware of an untapped market for photographs of personalities and scenes relevant to Welsh life. He not only worked from his studio base, producing thousands of cartes-de-visite, but notably travelled widely in north and mid-Wales photographing all kinds of scenes and persons, especially those with nonconformist connections.

Three thousand of his best negatives were purchased by Sir O.M. Edwards, a fervent supporter of the Welsh language and Welsh way of life, for use in his magazine Cymru. *These negatives, an insider's view, were later donated to the National Library of Wales and now provide us with some of the finest images available of late Victorian life in Wales.*

John Thomas's work spanned the era of wet collodion through to the next major development, that of the 'dry plate' which was invented during the 1880s by Dr R.L. Maddox. The gelatine dry plate was much easier to store and process than the wet plate, and most importantly, dramatically reduced exposure times. During much the same period, a new and improved printing medium – gelatine bromide paper – was also devised. The advanced process drew a new generation into the photographic tradition, among them many of the photographers represented in this volume. A great many photographers – amateur and professional – visited Wales, drawn by the magnificent scenery and the ease of travel on the ever-expanding rail system. Their work, in general, tends to concentrate on the 'picturesque Wales' of the tourist and thereby bypasses ordinary life and humanity in search of the perfect waterfall, sweeping sea view, or romantic castle ruin.

To discover the people of Wales, their daily preoccupations and culture, we generally have to search beyond the picturesque view of the traveller and look to the work of the local professional photographer. By recording the faces, places and character of their locality, often over a long period of time, they expand upon the insider's view and provide a reasonably rounded representation of the society to which they belonged. The photographs in this volume draw mainly from the collections of thousands of glass plate negatives now held at the National Library of Wales. Added to these are pictures taken by some travelling photographers and, inevitably, a number by unknown practitioners, their labour recorded for posterity, but their names lost with the passage of time.

Conwy. John Thomas

Chapter 2

INDUSTRY AND COMMERCE

By 1900 a clear majority of the Welsh people were urban dwellers. Industry had transformed the face of the country and relocated large numbers of its inhabitants from the rural areas to the towns. The central development of these years was the enormous growth of the south Wales coalfield. Its varied population changed the complexion of Welsh society as a whole, a fact demonstrated by the startling statistic that the two counties of Glamorgan and Monmouthshire in the south-east were home to 63 per cent of the total Welsh population by 1911.

Of all the industrial valleys of south Wales it is the Rhondda which is most closely associated with coalmining in the public's mind. Earlier in the twentieth century tourists visiting the area had celebrated the valley's unsullied natural beauty and its picturesque views were recorded in picture and prose. The transformation caused by industrialisation was more complete in that locality than in any other part of Wales. With fewer than 1,000 inhabitants in 1851, the narrow valley became a boisterous community – or rather, a series of communities strung out cheek-by-jowl along its length – of 153,000 souls by 1911. However, new employment opportunities and the greater personal freedoms which characterised life in the coalfield are not the whole story. Coalmining's development was punctuated with sickening regularity by tragic disasters which often claimed hundreds of lives at a time: the worst incident occurred in the hitherto obscure village of Senghennydd in 1913 when 439 men were killed.

The ports of the south Wales coast differed appreciably from the towns of the coalfield. Cardiff, Newport, Swansea, and Barry all flourished on the back of coal exports and developed a coherent middle-class presence which was absent from the one-industry coalmining settlements. Cardiff, which was granted city status in 1905, became the de facto national capital, a claim underlined by the grandeur of the new civic buildings of Cathays Park with their combination of classical and baroque architecture.

However, the numerical dominance of south-east Wales should not blind us to the existence of industrial centres elsewhere in the country. A highly distinctive society came into being in the slate-quarrying areas of north-west Wales where the workers toiled in circumstances as dangerous to their health as the coal mines, if not more so. Industrial and urban Wales confronted its inhabitants with a mixture of opportunities for economic advancement and the near certainty of a truncated life.

St Mary Street, Cardiff, c. 1905. Grosvenor Series postcard

Foundry workers, Aberystwyth, c. 1895. Arthur Lewis

A GREAT CITY

In the gigantic enterprise of our times, most of the great cities are too much concerned with their trade to pay too much attention to the health, comfort, pleasure, and recreation of the citizens, but Cardiff is an exception.

There is probably no modern city – at any rate, there is no great modern commercial city – which takes so much care of the municipal side of life, or has brought to greater perfection the many-sided projects that go to make up the corporate life of a great city.

Cardiff is essentially a well-kept and a well-governed city. The visitor comes to it under the impression that he will find a city black with the sins of its coal trade, that its streets will be dirty and ill-kept, and that such a place would be the last in the world where he would expect to find an illustration of the ideals embodied in the programme of the municipal reformer. But he soon finds his pre-conceived notions scattered before the reality.

'The Chicago of Wales: Cardiff's Municipal and Commercial Life', *Mayfair*, October 1912

FIRE AND GUNPOWDER

One of the hardest tasks the Cardiff Fire Brigade has had for some time was performed on Saturday night. About seven o'clock smoke was seen issuing from the ship chandlery stores of Messrs. Jones and Co., 145, Bute-road, and an alarm was quickly raised. The Central Fire Station was communicated with from the No. 5 alarm-box, whilst a messenger ran to the Bute-road Police-station. A reel was at once despatched from the latter place in charge of Fireman Lawrence, and a hose was quickly attached to a hydrant. A few minutes later the steam fire engine, Fire Queen, in charge of Chief Engineer Green arrived, and another couple of hoses were quickly at work. The supply of water was ample, but the greatest difficulty was experienced in finding a vantage point from which to combat the flames, as the fire had by this time obtained a very strong hold on the premises. . . . The ground and first floors were stocked with ship's stores, cordage, and other materials of a very inflammable description. The brigade, under the command of Mr W. Mckenzie, the head-constable, and Inspector Durston, first directed their efforts to this portion of the premises, and played upon the flames through windows

Firemen, c. 1898. Arthur Lewis

Aberystwyth fire brigade, c. 1905. Arthur Lewis

LOSSES THROUGH FIRE

The value of property lost through fire stands thus:–

	£
The United Kingdom	9,100,000
France	3,200,000
Germany	6,100,000
Russia	21,000,000
Belgium	500,000
Scandinavia	1,000,000
The United States	22,500,000
Canada	4,100,000

Almanac y Miloedd, 1896 (trans.)

THE CROWDED VALLEYS

which had to be broken in. The real seat of the fire could not be attacked by this means, however, and . . . the flames burst through the roof and began to extend to the shop. A couple of hoses were then taken to the front of the building and one was taken into the shop, and the fire there was quickly extinguished. The other hose was taken to the roof of the adjoining house, and from here the water was poured down into the flames, which were bursting through the roof of the warehouse and attacking the main building. It was quite evident, however, that not much of the warehouse could be saved, but from every point possible the fire was assailed, and after a while the efforts of the brigade were rewarded, and by about 8.30 the flames were under control. But it took until ten o'clock to completely extinguish the conflagration. The warehouse was gutted, and the back portion of the house was also burnt through. It was found after the fire had been extinguished that about 10 lb. of gunpowder was stored in a safe in the attic at the top of the house.

'Serious Fire at Cardiff', *Western Mail*, 7 February 1898

All the other British coalfields have fairly level or gently undulating surfaces. In South Wales the coalfield used to be spoken of as the 'hills', the earlier development having been on the higher land of the outcrop – but of more recent years 'the valleys' is the commonly-accepted synonym. Scooped out by the impetuous streams which start from the central mountain range of Brecknockshire, or one of its southern spurs, those valleys are for the most part extremely narrow, with inconveniently steep sides, some of them indeed being so narrow at some points that there is scarcely space enough on the level for main road and railway in addition to the river itself. Nevertheless, it is into these valleys, shut in on either side by high mountains that the mining population is crowded, and it is this same narrow space, and often right in

Tonypandy, c. 1905, possibly by Ladd

the midst of the dwelling houses that the surface works of the collieries and any by-product plants have also of necessity been placed.

Commission of Inquiry into Industrial Unrest: No. 7 Division, *Report of the Commissioners for Wales including Monmouthshire* (1917)

SUCH A CLEVER CHILD SHE WAS

I dare say I could write a book on my early struggles with my seven children, and a miner's home to contend with; and many a week my husband has not had a penny of a wage to bring home, besides the experience of three big strikes and many small ones.

I may say we were married nineteen years before we lost one, and then I lost my baby first, a grand little girl of two. Then, a year and a half later, I lost a fine lad of fourteen in the fever hospital, of scarlet fever and diphtheria. Two years after that we lost a girl of twelve from tubercular disease of the kidneys from cow's milk. The doctor was treating her for eight years for Bright's disease of the kidneys. I brought them up breast-fed, so she must have contracted it after she was weaned. Such a clever child she was. So you will see we have had our troubles.

Children in the studio of D.C. Harries

Baby Graves.

MERTHYR'S YEARLY TOLL TO HER INSANITARY DWELLINGS.

This means that hundreds of human lives are being sacrificed year after year in Dowlais and the other bad districts by the failure of the capitalists employing labour to rescue that labour from foul and filthy dwellings which are death-traps and murder-holes. . . . . Merthyr does not destroy its refuse but it destroys its children.—" Human Wales," by GEO. R. SIMS.

Baby graves. J.M. Staniforth, 1907

I may say I had very good times at confinements, except the first and last. The youngest was born feet first, which was an awful experience, and her heart was nearly stopped beating, so I think that left her heart weak, and she cut her teeth with bronchitis. I used to get her up always by the ninth day until the last. I was between forty-one and forty-two when she was born, so had to rest a bit longer, but had to see to household duties as soon as possible.

Margaret Llewelyn Davies (ed.), *Maternity: Letters from Working Women* (1915)

STENCH OF THE RIVER

The river contains a large proportion of human excrement, stable and pigsty manure, congealed blood, offal and entrails from the slaughterhouses, the rotten carcasses of animals, cats and dogs . . . old cast-off articles of clothing and bedding, and boots, bottles, ashes, street refuse and a host of other articles. . . . In dry weather the stench becomes unbearable.

Report of the Medical Officer of Health for the Rhondda Urban District Council, 1893

RENT RISES

There are few questions more important today than the housing question, seeing the way things are going on. Taking a walk last Saturday in a certain street, I came across a group of people discussing the raid the rack-renter had made on them that day. They had had a week's notice to quit and it was understood that the rent was to be raised and that it was with a vengeance. The houses that I refer to are owned by a

well known local landlord. The houses were a few months ago 11/– a month, they rose after to 13/– but now to 16/–. They have one room down and two up. Other small houses with one room up and one down have risen from 11/– to 16/– because the landlord has been forced by the inspector to do some repairs that were badly needed, the places being a nuisance and injurious to health. Tenants are afraid to ask for improvements, for the rent goes up when it is done or the tenant is turned out.

Merthyr Express, 19 May 1900

RHONDDA TRANSFORMED

What if the veterans of a century ago were permitted to see the swarming hosts of Glamorgan and Monmouthshire engaged in their respective occupations, with the black mineral pouring into the lap of Cardiff, Newport, Swansea and Llanelli, where the argosies of the nations await its arrival to convey it to the remotest parts of the earth? What if they saw the transformation of the Rhondda valley from a sleepy hollow into the most active and thriving community of Great Britain or the world?

Western Mail, 1 January 1901

CATASTROPHE AT THE COLLIERY

I shall never forget my first impression of a great colliery disaster (wrote a *Western Mail* reporter soon after arrival at the scene on Tuesday morning) when a special train brought a little party of us along side the pit this morning. Men, hatless, coatless, and breathless, were rushing hither and thither, carrying stretchers, linen, boards, and everything they could lay their hands to, working at the utmost pressure, yet with the greatest method. Bound about this ill-fated colliery were thousands of dry eyed, sad faced men, women, and children, watching patiently every stretcher as it was brought to the surface.

Then they went quietly to the coverlet, lifted one corner, and turned away with a sigh of relief or a groan.

There were twelve corpses then in the mortuary. God only knows how many more would be there before nightfall. Down at the Aber-hall nurses and medical men were working like heroines and heroes among the injured. They were mostly cases of severe burning, and in a few cases bruises and cuts.

Everyone was asking, 'What about those poor 400 still down the pit?'

I put the same question to one of the colliery officials. 'God only knows,' he said: 'they may be safe, they may be all dead. We have got to wait until we can kill the fire away down there, and then we shall know more than we do now.'

Down in this Lancaster pit the catastrophe had its conception. Just 935 men went down on the morning shift. Shortly before 8.30 that terrible blast, heard even beyond Caerphilly, had shattered the top of the frame work and

Senghennydd Pit disaster, postcard no. 6. Benton of Glasgow

Mines rescue team, 1913 (detail)

Senghennydd Pit disaster (right), postcard no. 15. Benton of Glasgow

Daio Jenkins from the Rhondda Look You !.

Postcard view of a miner, posted in 1927. The lantern shows that the photograph was probably taken much earlier.

OUTPUT OF THE COLLIERIES

The output of the Collieries at various periods has been:–

	Tons
1864	400,000
1880	750,000
1885	1,381,000
1890	1,305,000
1895	1,485,000
1900	1,942,000
1905	2,741,000
1910	3,219,000
1911	3,443,000
1912	3,503,000
1913	3,874,000

DESCRIPTIONS OF COALS MARKETED BY THE POWELL DUFFRYN STEAM COAL COMPANY LIMITED

Powell Duffryn Large Steam Coal:–
A smokeless mixture from the Collieries in the Aberdare and Rhymney Valleys. On the British and Foreign Admiralty Lists.

Best Large Steam Coal:–
A smokeless coal specially prepared for use in steam motor wagons, and supplied for this purpose to customers in all parts of England and Wales.

Paris Nuts:–
A washed smokeless coal ranging from 1¼ in. to 2½ in. in size and extracted from the coal raised from the Collieries in the Aberdare Valley. It is specially prepared for the French market.

Aberdare Washed Beans:–
A washed smokeless coal from ⅜ in. to 1¼ in. in size, extracted from Aberdare Valley coal and used for steam raising.

Aberdare Washed Peas:–
A similar coal to Aberdare Washed Beans, but of smaller size, viz. from ⅛ in. to ⅜ in. and used for much the same purpose.

Aberdare Washed Grains:–
These are similar in description to Aberdare Washed Peas, but of still smaller size, and range from ³⁄₁₆ in. to ⅛ in.

Aberdare Washed Duff:–
A fine coal all below ³⁄₁₆ in. in size.

Aberdare Unwashed Duff:–
Similar to Aberdare Washed Duff in size and other respects, but not washed. It is very largely used for patent fuel manufacture.

[Other coals listed are New Tredegar Washed Nuts, New Tredegar Washed Peas, New Tredegar Washed Duff, New

winding wheel, and killed one of the banksmen working there – John Moggeridge of Senghenydd – and seriously injured the other, John Morgan. Approximately, there were 600 men in the York pit and 435 in the Lancaster. Nearly all the York men were all right, and 90 per cent of them did not know anything had happened until they were called to the surface.

I spoke to one white-faced young lad, who had just come up, and asked him what were the chances of the Lancaster men. 'My God,' he said, 'the pit is burning like a furnace. They will never get those men out alive!' They were at least getting one or two now and again, and bringing them via the York Pit up the shaft there.

But still the stretchers were busy. There were corpses and injured men coming up every five minutes. How these colliers worked for their stricken fellows! I was told that all the officials had gone down. . . . By-and-bye they began to take down canaries to test the air below, but it was no good – more work had to be done before they could reach the 400 entombed men in the Lancaster Pit.

Western Mail, 15 October 1913

Tredegar Colliery Small Coal, Aberdare Colliery Small Coal, White Rose Large Coal, White Rose Cobbles, White Rose Small Coal, Foundry and Furnace Coke, Coke Screenings, Boulets.]

The Powell Duffryn Steam Coal Company Limited, 1864–1914

TWELFTH BIRTHDAY – FIRST DAY DOWN THE PIT

All the boys in school looked forward with longing to the day when they would be allowed to begin work. Release from the boredom of school might have influenced them; but my happiness was not so much in leaving school as in the idea of actually going to work underground. We saw the pit boys coming home in their black clothes, with black hands and faces, carrying their food-boxes, drinking tins, and gauze-lamps. They adopted an air of superiority to mere schoolboys. We humbly bowed to this. They had experienced danger amidst thundering falls of roof, and had mysterious adventures, in deeps, levels and headings with blue balloons of gas threatening to explode around their lamps. They associated with big men and wonderful horses. They earned six shillings and ninepence every week. Never would one of them dream of giving up the pits. Life began to be worth living when once they had gone down.

My eagerness to go down the pit was so great that as soon as I came home, I interviewed Dai Morgan the overman of Navigation Colliery, on my own initiative, and showed him my qualifications: I should be twelve years of age on the following day and had entirely satisfied Parliament that my education was complete. He said:

'Right you arr, Kaet'n.'

Next morning, I was up at half past five. It was a grey, sunless morning, but I was thrilling with happiness, and I could scarcely sit peacefully at the table to take my breakfast of bread and butter and tea without milk.

My mother put my food in a small tin box and filled a tin 'jack' with cold tea, and said 'May the Lord bring you safe home!' as I left the house.

I went to the pit-head in an ecstasy – the colliery was just behind our house – with a thousand men and boys, amidst iron trams, iron tracks, grease and machinery. I was given a long gauze-lamp, called a 'sprag', entered the pit-cage and, crushed in between about a dozen boys and men, was lowered into the darkness. The swift descent took my breath away and I gasped with fright and clung to my friends' dusty clothes.

Colliers at the Pantyffynnon Colliery rising to the surface. D.C. Harries

'Lord of Penmachno' (Arglwydd Penmachno), a slate splitter in the 1880s. John Thomas

That first descent into Navigation coal pit, at half past six o'clock, on the morning of my twelfth birthday, April 16, 1883, interested me wonderfully. As we dropped below the brink of the shaft, the pale daylight seemed to spring upwards and vanish like a flying ghost. For a moment after that I could see nothing at all. Then faint yellow rays appeared from our lamps, and I could see as well as feel the forms of men and boys with me.

They had ranged themselves in two lines against the iron sides of the 'carriage', as they called it. Each man and boy had his hand raised, clinging to a bar. One of the men lifted my hand to a bar and said good-humouredly:

'Ketch by here, wassy; or you'll tumble out, p'raps.'

All were kind to a beginner. They could tell by my schoolboy clothes that this was my first day in the mine.

We were going down so rapidly – the pit was a quarter of a mile deep – that our lamplight seemed to me to be always running up.

All the time a terrific wind kept shrieking and blowing bits of coal into our faces. The tiny, flying things struck my forehead and cheeks sharply and painfully. I felt as if I were falling through the earth.

The quarter of a minute, which was all the time taken for the quarter of a mile drop, had been a magical period in which I had passed from happiness to terror, and back again from terror to happiness. I was delighted to be in the pit.

There seemed to be a kind of distinction about it which made me think I was doing something very fine. I was especially proud of being with men and horses. The good humoured voices of men and boys, as they tramped slowly inwards, their laughter, snatches of song, and lively chatter, the neighing of animals, jingle of harness, and thud of hoofs in the dust, gave me a feeling of real happiness.

'Kaet'n,' Jim said, 'you shall go with Darling. Take care of yourself now, mind you. She is nasty sometimes. Tom Pugh!' he shouted, to the darkness beyond. 'Joe Kaet'n will door with you.'

'Darling' was a little brown mare with one flashing eye and a red hole where the other eye ought to have been. She had run wild once too often in the pit, and had knocked the eye out by colliding with a tram of coal which was in her way. Tom Pugh was her driver, and I was now her door-boy.

All that day I followed Darling and her vagaries. I rode behind on the coal trams which she pulled. When she stopped at a door I ran ahead, opened it, and stood by it, like my lady's page, while she and her load passed through. Then I closed the door and had another ride behind.

Dinner-time came, and I sat with the other boys on the ground, in soft, black dust which was very comfortable. Under a timbered roof, we opened our food boxes. My bread and cheese, and the tea from my 'jack', had a sweeter taste that day than any food or drink I had ever taken. Rats were running impatiently up and down the dark roadside anxious to get the crumbs. We could see the rats' eyes sometimes. They were like sparks of fire in the blackness.

We did not recommence work for a quarter of an hour after dinner. We took a 'spell'. I stretched myself at full length in the dust as the others did, and we talked on some

Quarrymen at the Bonc Shaft, 1913

interesting subjects. A rat ran over my face, and the touch of its smooth, cold, little feet on my cheeks made me shiver with fright, and I sat up. The other boys laughed. I soon got used to the rats.

I wanted to be seen going home with the men from the pit, black, vividly black, so black as to be nearly invisible.

My wish was granted. I was seen by most of my friends in my black clothes, with my face black, my hands black, and my pit-lamp and 'box-and-jack' black, as I came home. My mother smiled at my comical appearance as I went into the house. But there was a sigh in her smile.

Joseph Keating, *My Struggle for Life* (1916)

TRYING TO EARN A LIVING

Tomos, in his stall far down and in under the mountains, with his lamp swinging at his belt, was testing the coal with his mandrel. He had stripped himself to the waist, as the place was warm. A forest of posts held up the roof, which was so low that he was bent almost in double beneath it. He had worked in the Cragwyn mine since he was a boy of seven and knew every subtle characteristic of coal, as far as getting it out of its bed was concerned. Each swing of his pick was the stroke of a master craftsman. His mandrel was the inspired tool of an artist achieving the complete expression of an idea. He cut skilfully. Yet when the big slip came down, it crumbled as if it were only black flour. Tomos, coughing in the cloud of dust, swore at the heap of rottenness. He wanted big lumps for his tram, but could only see two or three bits like pickled walnuts in the dust on the ground. He tried again at another slip. His task was troublesome, owing to the impossibility of cutting out any large pieces, and he frequently paused to gaze in sorrow at the seam, with his lamp held close to it. The face did not shine under the rays as good coal would have done. It looked dull and dismal. It had all the jointures and sections of coal formation. But when the sharp points of the mandrel touched it, it shuddered and broke as if it were nothing but solidified mud veined with slag and bast that stretched across it like rows of old wounds on a black man's cheek.

'Is it worth while trying to earn a living in the Cragwyn pit?' Tomos was asking himself seriously, as all pay depended on the number of tons of solid coal he sent out.

Joseph Keating, *Flower of the Dark* (1917)

TO DIE YOUNG

My first impression regarding Welsh quarrymen is that their hard lot produces premature decay and old age – very frequently affecting particular tissues, often causing a general withering. God turns them out a very even lot as babies; look at them above sixty as they pour out of a large quarry, and pray that the Almighty may give them sense and knowledge to understand what has produced the awful change.

. . . how terribly numerous are the tubercular class of affliction that produces their premature death and how frequently they die when a well fed man would recover. I will not enlarge to you on these points . . . it seems to be their lot to die young of consumptive diseases, while their English masters die of gout and apoplexy, with white hair and rubicund faces above sixty.

John Roberts to John William, 7 January 1890

WELSH WERE TOUGHER

After the Cornishmen had tried their best to match the Welshmen, they had to give up the hard graft two by two, with the Welshmen taking their places. The supervisor would take special note of the work of the English and the Welsh, and he agreed that the Welsh were tougher people for hard work. Within a few months, there was not one Englishman working in the hole, and only two remained of all the Cornishmen, and those were on board the steam engine, where the work was light.

Hunangofiant Chwarelwr (Autobiography of a Quarryman), Cymru, 1900 (trans.)

The slate quay at Caernarfon, c. 1910. Arthur Lewis

Penrhyn v Parry commemorative photograph of the Defence Committee, 1903. Wickens

TEA: THE CAUSE OF INDIGESTION?

It is the habit of the quarrymen in this district to send a boy about half an hour before the meal time to an eating house, prepared by the owners for their comfort, with tea and sugar and water in the same kettle, which is put on the fire and boiled. It then stews there half an hour or more before the men come there to drink it. That habit, continued day after day for a number of years, is in my opinion the cause of the indigestion we find in this district, and other diseases which come as a consequence. They undoubtedly ought to have two kettles. They ought to boil the water in one and brew it in the other. I have been trying to preach this to them for a long time, but they will not be advised on that point.

Report by the Quarry Committee of Inquiry on slate quarrying in Merionethshire, 1893

LORD PENRHYN CHARGED WITH TYRANNY

We have received from Lord Penrhyn's manager a printed report of an address delivered by him to the men now at work in the quarries on Monday. . . . Lord Penrhyn has not been and cannot be vindicated of the charges of tyranny and injustice brought against him by Mr Parry while he maintains his present arrogant attitude and denies to the workmen of Bethesda the right to earn their living by their own labour. . . .

Lord Penrhyn will entertain no proposals for reinstating the whole of the men on any terms, and that he will agree to nothing but absolute and unconditional surrender. . . . That is precisely the attitude we should have expected Lord Penrhyn to adopt and for the would-be arbitrators to have their labour for their pains. Of course Lord Penrhyn is actuated by nothing but concerns for the interest of the workmen themselves. That has been his guiding influence in all his actions; in his refusing to deal with the men through their representatives; in getting rid of men who acted as spokesmen for themselves and their fellows; in distributing rewards to the 'loyalists'; in all this he only had the interest of the men at heart. . . .

They are all the same, these capitalist autocrats, these union-smashers . . . it is always for the benefit of the men themselves that they seek to destroy the baneful despotism of the men's organisation. And the beneficent effect is – of their action, when successful, is at once seen, as at Bethesda, where, as Lord Penrhyn says: 'The thousand men and boys are like a happy family in their relation with officials and their employer.' . . .

It is rather strange, however, that the men who are out should prefer to endure privation and suffering rather than share the pleasant conditions which have given contentment to the 'happy family'. But there they are, and the question now is what is to become of them and what is to be done for them. . . . In the meantime the trade unions should bestir themselves to defeat Lord Penrhyn's plan of campaign, which is to starve the men into absolute submission and individual surrender.

Justice, 4 April 1903

Building Port Talbot Docks, 1898

OFF TO JOIN THE NAVVIES

At this period, an invasion of navvies overwhelmed Mountain Ash. They were cutting, digging, and shovelling all through the valley. They had horses, wagons and windlasses. Deep, narrow gullies made in fields by hundreds of navvies, and the sight of fresh clay they threw up on each side, captivated me.

A few of my elder intimates had succeeded in getting appointments as 'nippers'. They received six or seven shillings a week. I absolutely yearned to become a 'nipper' and to be a real navvy. There was brilliant romance in tramping from place to place with the admired gang.

My love for the toiling rovers – they were fine, tall men, clean-looking, in moleskin trousers and pilot jackets, and swung their great, anchor-like picks and shovels with an easy rhythm – was so strong that while school holidays were on I rose at half-past five, just as the navvies did, tied some food up in a red handkerchief, as they did, and went out to the cutting in fields or hillside at six o'clock, as they did. From six to half-past eight I took an active part in the work, like an unsalaried Parliamentary secretary, hitching a horse to wagons which the navvies filled with clay. At half-past eight the ganger sang out 'Ye-ho, boys', and we 'knocked off', sat on the grass, untied our red handkerchiefs and ate our 'tommy' in the morning sunshine with mountains in front and behind us.

The navvies were always in good-humour and full of laughable stories. Their intelligence was astonishing. They never lacked a subject. They were artists in human conversation and geniality. They accepted my companionship as that of an equal. Entire independence seemed to be the natural thing for them to feel.

Joseph Keating, *My Struggle for Life* (1916)

THE VILLAGE SHOP

I find it difficult to convey the central and dominating place occupied by the Old Shop in the life of a small community like that of Rhymney. It was, to begin with, a commodious, solid and stately building, standing in its own grounds, served by its own railway lines, with accommodation for grocery, drapery, ironmongery, furniture, butchery, and baking departments, a slaughter house, stables, warehouse and offices. It was admirably planned and equipped for its purpose as a general store. To a small boy it was a wonderland of romance.

Pulleys raised sacks of flour to the top storey; men in white uniforms stood in a row at the big counter, one weighing tea from great chests on a square of paper fast enough to keep two or three others folding and packing; the cool and spotless butchery with stone floors sprinkled over with fresh sawdust held the carcasses of great beasts hanging from the beams. But best of all was the snug warmth of the stables with the chestnut cobs and ponies, the scent of the leather and polished harness, and the rattling of the halter chains, the clatter of hooves on the cobbled floor, and the feel of the corn in the bins which I let slip through my fingers like a rosary.

In Pay Week when the overdue wages were adjusted there would be very brisk business and the large assembly hall of the grocery department would be full of working women shopping. It was a sociable, talkative crowd, full of rude fun and banter in good times and of pluck and patience in bad. Many would be nursing babies in shawls tightly drawn around their bulbous bosoms and swaying hips. Pregnancy was perpetual with the majority. A mouthful of good teeth was a rare sight and here and there one saw a pock-marked face. . . . There were the frugal who feared to get into debt and the debauched who never expected to get out of debt. Babies, weddings, funerals, strikes and lock-outs were the original sources of debt, and drink was an unfailing fountain. 'Hen Gownt' (old account) was the euphemism for long-standing debt and some families stood in the books owing eighty or a hundred pounds. . . .

Thomas Jones, *Rhymney Memories* (1938)

FLOWER OF SULPHUR, THE ELIXIR OF LIFE

I was born and reared at a house – now a shop – in the main road and shopping centre of our Welsh village. At the end of the street about thirty feet from the house was a cinder tip eighty feet high surrounded by a boundary wall. On the outside of the wall running parallel with the public road was an open brook. This was part of our playground. At one end of the street facing this brook was a chemist's shop and at the other end a grocer's shop. The chemist's window showed the customary large coloured bottles – blue, green and red – I think they are professionally called carboys – and were the Trade mark of all chemists in those days; they proclaimed the nature of the business as do the brass balls over the pawnshop and the striped pole outside the barber's. Behind the counter stood the chemist, a tall good-looking bachelor with handle bar moustache, he was courteous, reserved and a man of few words; I never knew him to have any intimate friends or acquaintances. After business hours he retired into strict seclusion . . . the manufacturing chemist business was in its early infancy if it had yet been born. The only advert I can recall is an oil reputed to cure rheumatism; lumbago, sciatica and neuritis all went under that one name. The next best seller was Kernick pills to cure everything. The chemist stock was very simple and consisted mainly of Salts, Spanish, Sticking Plaster and Flowers of Sulphur. People had been taught that a spring cleaning of the body once a year was as essential as spring cleaning of the house. Women talked and

Interior of a grocery shop, probably at Llandeilo. D.C. Harries

Star Supply Stores, Garnant. D.C. Harries. The photograph was taken after the shopkeeper had been brutally murdered in 1921

The Luther Bye Pharmacy in Ammanford. D.C. Harries

Lipton's shop, Ammanford, c. 1910. D.C. Harries

declared very knowingly that children must have Flowers of Sulphur once a year, because they get new blood every spring. The process of applying this Elixir of Life might form an excellent subject for the cartoonist. Flower of Sulphur is a saffron yellow powder, and had to be mixed with treacle. Sop mixed, it went by the name of Brimstone and Treacle; good word brimstone. . . . This particular treacle which accompanied the sulphur was a cross between molasses and coal tar; a black-brown thick product. The mixture now ready, mother would come armed with a basin and a dessert spoon. As the spoon filled and mother approached, I, poor victim, backed away until I was up against the nearest wall. The crisis reached, no further possibility of retreat, I was seized by the scruff and ordered to open my mouth, then I received the full contents of that accursed spoon and warned that if I persisted in this obstinacy I would get two spoonfuls next time. It was effective; at any rate I know it did the Spring Cleaning.

Edmund Stonelake, *The Autobiography of Edmund Stonelake* (1981)

CAERPHILLY CHEESES AND OLD ACCOUNTS

We lived for years behind and above our busy shop; a living room, pantry and scullery behind, three bedrooms above. It was a 'credit' shop and a history of family fortunes. On a lectern desk panelled with a frosted glass screen lay an enormous black ledger, six inches thick, a double page for each customer. Its chronicle of strike-time debts was my mother's bible and bane, and in my mind it remained the Ledger of Old Accounts, durable as a lichened tombstone. . . .

The shop smelled of wholesome things. Golden sawdust, thrown fresh every morning on the swept floor between the two long parallel counters, retained its breath of sawn trees. There was one chair, for stout old women panting on arrival from up or down hilly Clydach in our wonderful bad weather. There were lettered canisters of black and gold, an odorous coffee-grinding machine, mounds of yellow Canadian and pallid Caerphilly cheeses, rosy cuts of ham and bacon, wide slabs of butter cut by wire for the scales, and bladders of lard. Behind the counter over which my mother presided stretched wall-fixtures stacked with crimson packets

Alberto & Lupi ice-cream van, also used as a chip van during the winter, selling hot food to the miners of the Great Mountain Colliery, Tumble. The two-cylinder van was coachbuilt in Tumble and painted in Llanelli. D.C. Harries

Bridgend market, c. 1905

of tea, blue satchels of sugar, vary-coloured bags of rice, dried fruits and peas, weighed and packaged by hand out of chests and canvas sacks on quiet Monday. Soaps gave their own clean smell. Especially the favoured kind which arrived in long bars and, cut into segments, was used both for scrubbing houses and washing pit-dirt from colliers' backs and fronts. Slabs of rich cake lay in a glass case on an interesting counter stacked with biscuit tins. Packets of Ringer's tobacco, black chewing shag, spices, almonds and dried herbs occupied a row of drawers under a counter, though not in the one always chosen by our cat for her frequent *accouchements*, filling me with wonder that she could force her heavy body through the narrow aperture at the back; an intelligent puss, she accepted the quick drowning of her load with experienced resignation and plodded on to the next adventure. . . .

Rhys Davies, *Print of a Hare's Foot* (1969)

MOTHER WAS MORE THAN A MATCH FOR ANY MAN

It was approaching eleven o'clock when another lodger-customer, a bantam man swollen with Saturday-night bombast lurched into the shop. Several excrescences always on his inflamed face had caused him to be nicknamed Jenkins warts. A thickset, two-rooted beetroot of a man, for a moment he

eyed the debonair Gentleman collier with a lurking belligerence, suddenly gripped a fistful of his velvet jacket and gave him a push against the counter, behind which my mother stood. Years of exasperation against bad times, unpaid debts and meagerly rewarded hard work galvanised my mother. Before her lay the day-book, a sizeable volume from which the unpaid cash totals of daily purchases were transferred to the sombre ledger of Old Accounts. She lifted the book in both hands, leaned forward, and brought it down smartly on the bantam's capped head. 'Out!' she pointed a finger to the door. He slunk away at once, struck by a woman!

The Gentleman collier adjusted his tugged jacket into its former drape. 'Gone too far even for the Salvation Army, poor chap!' he observed. My mother took a pencil from her coiled hair and reopened the day-book. 'Let me see, that clears up everything for your week, doesn't it? Eighteen shillings and four pence.' She was as instantaneous with sums as with logical deduction.

Rhys Davies, *Print of a Hare's Foot* (1969)

THE LATHER BOY

My first job, when I was about eight years old, was lather boy in a barber's shop. I was so small I had to stand on a stool to do the job, and I worked from 8 a.m. on Saturday to 1 a.m.

Hairdressing salon in south Wales. D.C. Harries

on Sunday. Many of the customers used to come in drunk. One night I got fed up and I ran out saying, 'I'm not staying here any more.' Then I took a job with a grocer. I used to take a truck loaded with groceries to the farms around Merthyr from 6 p.m. Friday till nine or ten o'clock, and then from 8 a.m. Saturday till 1 a.m. Sunday. I got half a crown a week for that.

Arthur Horner, *Incorrigible Rebel* (1960)

STRIKERS ON THE RAMPAGE

Riotous scenes, without a parallel in the South Wales Coalfield, were enacted last night in mid-Rhondda and at Aberaman. At both places, the police and the mob were in fierce conflict for many hours, charge after charge being made by the constabulary upon the infuriated crowd. In the mid-Rhondda alone over a hundred casualties are reported, injured strikers being conveyed in batches to local surgeries for treatment. There were 60 casualties at Aberaman, and both there and in mid-Rhondda many members of the police force were struck by huge missiles, not a few sustaining serious injury.

In the mid-Rhondda district the first outbreak of disorder took place in the afternoon at Tonypandy and Llwynypia. A mob of young men were charged by police who, using their batons, drove them off, leaving six on the highway injured.

These as quickly as possible received first aid, and were subsequently removed home. Later in the evening there were grave developments at Tonypandy. Time after time police and strikers came into serious conflicts, and the riots that ensued were the most serious witnessed within living memory in the coalfield. First the strikers, repeating the demonstration of Monday night, attacked with showers of stone the Power Station of the Glamorgan Colliery. Repulsed by the police after a sanguinary baton charge, the strikers, reinforced, returned again to the attack, and were once again charged by mounted police, dozens being rendered prostrate by blows from police batons. Later the strikers, forming in procession, marched through the main streets of Tonypandy smashing the windows of scores of business establishments en route to Penygraig, and looting the contents of shop windows.

At Aberaman a combined attack was made on the Powell Duffryn washery. A mob of two thousand men joined in the assault, accompanied by a large number of women. The police were fiercely attacked, and some were seriously injured. The rioters climbed over the fencing and set fire to a quantity of straw stored in a railway wagon. Immediately there was a huge conflagration and expensive property was in imminent peril. Prompt rescue measures, however, were taken, and the fire was extinguished ere much damage had been done. The mob only yielded to a series of baton charges, and the crowd rushed pell mell along the canal bank, many being jostled into the canal.

Police gathering at 'The Rink', Tonypandy, during the disturbances of 1910/11

Worker's banner linking the 1911 disturbances and deaths to previous events

Last night a troop train conveyed two squadrons of the 18th Hussars from Tidworth to Cardiff, where they were quartered for the night, accommodation being found for them at the Barracks, ready at any moment to proceed to the scene of operations in the affected districts. Companies of the North Lancashires and the Lancashire Fusiliers, who had started from Tidworth Barracks in company with the Hussars, remained behind at Swindon. The Hussars, it is officially reported, were drafted into South Wales at the request of the Chief Constable of Glamorganshire, who communicated through the local military authorities an appeal for the assistance of two hundred cavalry and two companies of infantry in the protection of colliery property. In the early morning a troop of Hussars travelled from Swindon through Cardiff to Pontypridd.

At the time of going to press the turmoil had subsided, and quiet was being maintained throughout the disturbed areas.

South Wales Daily News, 9 November 1910

A FATAL STRIKE AT LLANELLI

Saturday will be for ever memorable in the history of Llanelly, for surely never was such a concentration of horrors crowded into a short twelve hours. The town had become panic-stricken, its busy streets have been invaded by troops, its inhabitants have been shot at by the soldiery, hooliganism has been rampant, and, to crown all, the incendiary has been at work with appalling results. All this took place between two o'clock in the afternoon and midnight, and, as may be imagined, it has created the deepest consternation in a community which has always been notable for law-abiding instincts of its inhabitants.

For several reasons Llanelly could not help being one of the storm centres of the railway strike. The Great Western Railway line is particularly vulnerable to attack. The two level-crossings which command the passenger station on either hand cross main streets and, except for the single gates, are not protected in any way. The result has been that since the strike commenced these crossings have been easily held by an unruly mob and traffic held up. A detachment of troops arrived on the scene on Friday morning. Later in the day more troops appeared, and the place was cleared after the soldiers had fixed their bayonets and the Riot Act had been read.

On Saturday morning, as a measure of precaution, the magistrates decided to close all the public-houses in the vicinity at noon. Early in the afternoon a down train arrived at the station, after having negotiated the eastern crossing without difficulty. The western crossing, however, was held by a hostile crowd, and some time elapsed before the way

Street scene, Aberystwyth, 1910. Arthur Lewis

Mending miners' boots at Major's Boot Repair Depot, Ammanford or Pantyffynnon. D.C. Harries

could be cleared for the train to proceed. Some 250 yards beyond this point the train came to a standstill, and immediately there was a fusillade of stones from the crowd which lined the slopes on each side of the permanent way. The train was boarded by some of the bolder spirits, and efforts made to get the driver and fireman off the footplate. This brought up the men of the Worcester Regiment at the double with their rifles. It was not anticipated that the soldiers would have much trouble in dealing with the crowd, but a heavy stone striking one of the men in khaki on the head seems to have roused their tempers, for a minute later they raised their rifles, and a volley rang through the air. This was quickly followed by two further volleys. In the confusion that followed it was seen that four men had been shot, two of them with fatal results.

The victims of the shooting are:–

John Jones (22), of Railway-terrace, tin-plate worker, killed.
Leonard Worsall, of London, lodging at 16, High-Street, killed.
John Francis, Nelson-terrace, wound in the throat, now lying at hospital.
Benjamin Hambury, Railway-terrace, wound on the hand.

The victims of this occurrence were not among the crowd of strikers at all. They were standing in gardens which abut the line. The troops declared that their intention was to avoid the crowd by shooting in the air, but several eye-witnesses do not hesitate to describe the deplorable affair as reckless shooting under circumstances which did not call for resort to such an extreme measure.

Western Mail, 21 August 1911

NOW IT'S US AND THEM

I. The old policy of identity of interest between employers and ourselves be abolished, and a policy of open hostility installed . . .

XIX. That our objective be to build up an organisation, that will ultimately take over the mining industry and carry it on in the interests of the workers.

The Miners' Next Step (1912)

COAL EXPORTED FROM NEWPORT TO THE WORLD

Newport is one of the three largest coal exporting ports in the world, holding records for quick despatch which are unsurpassed. The Newport docks possess the finest single sheet of water of any in the country. It has, indeed, been claimed in the press that the new extension gives Newport the largest single dock in the world. . . . The proximity of the port to the South Wales coalfield is another valuable feature, as coal can be purchased locally at 3d per ton less than it costs elsewhere. The coal from this district is admitted to be the best and most economical in the world for heat-producing and steam-raising,

and millions of tons are exported annually. Battleships of many navies are bunkered with it, and it is regularly used by railway and steamship companies at home and abroad. . . . The import and export trade of the port has gone up by leaps and bounds. During 1908 it amounted to 7,362,818 tons. This was over one million tons more than three years previously.

Edward S. Hadley, 'Newport: The Port and its Great Docks', *Great Western Railway Magazine*, Vol. XXI (1909)

NAMES OF COALS

The yard coal of Glamorgan is invariably of the same thickness throughout. In Rhymney it is the 'gloyr coch', or red coal; in Tredegar, the 'gloyr ehyd'. The four-feet of Glamorgan is known at Rhymney as black coal, or 'gloyr du'; at Tredegar and Sirhowy as 'gloyr mawr', and at these places it is about six feet. The six feet coal at Dowlais, Rhymney, and Tredegar is really from nine feet to ten feet thick. The nine feet, known as 'Rhas Las', is thicker at Dowlais and Cyfarthfa than anywhere else. The lower four feet averages two to four feet. The yard coal is three feet at Cyfarthfa, but from Penydarren to Nantyglo four feet.

Charles Wilkins, *Coal* (1888)

Cardiff Docks, 1906. Francis Frith & Co.

Steam crane at the building of Port Talbot Docks, 1898

TRADES UNION PIONEERS

The New Flint Miners refused to work because the employers failed to pay wages. They had been for weeks without receiving full wages. Sometimes they would get a sub on Saturday, other Saturdays no pay at all. They refused to work, consequently the mine was closed, and the men had to find work elsewhere.

The members of Bettisfield Lodge have been very unfortunate, something wrong almost throughout the year. The employer who failed at New Flint Colliery got the Bettisfield Colliery, with some others, and we have not had a week's peace since this new company was formed. We hope that in a short time we shall be able to agree to a price list, which is now under consideration, then we may expect better things from Bettisfield. You will find that £1,938 14s 1d has been paid in strikes and lock-outs during the year. You have granted the Bethesda Quarry-men on strike £200, although it is not what we have promised them; we promised them £25 per month. The heavy items which we have paid at home is our reason for not sending the £25 per month, hoping to be able to continue our support from this time out. The Bethesda Quarry-men are fighting a battle for the trades union world, and should be well supported.

Denbighshire and Flintshire Miners' Federation Report, 1903

Steering a passage around the north Wales coast

Chapter 3

RURAL SOCIETY

I
f the most visible social changes occurred in the towns, the countryside was not immune to the impact of the modern world either. In the late nineteenth century deferential attitudes to the gentry melted away in the face of democratic reforms which undermined the age-old political power of the landed class, depriving them of leadership in the community. As an Anglicised, Conservative and Anglican class in a Welsh and predominantly Nonconformist and Liberal society, the gentry were an isolated and despised minority with few resources at their disposal to re-establish their waning authority. As more men acquired the right to vote, and the secret ballot afforded the individual protection from vindictive landlords and employers after 1872, there emerged a determination to challenge the political power of the gentry. With the creation of County Councils in 1888 the influence of the gentry in their localities was reduced even further. By the close of the century land was no longer the secure investment it had once been and landownership no longer guaranteed political influence and the respect of social inferiors. These developments prompted the owners of the great estates to begin to sell parcels of land in the years immediately preceding the First World War. The selling of land quickened after the end of the war and by the early 1920s vast

swathes of the country had been bought by those who farmed it, a transfer of land from one social class to another without precedent in Welsh history.

Ownership of the land continued to bestow some benefits and the tremors emanating from seismic social and political change did not immediately affect the pastimes of the gentry. Hunting remained popular among the privileged, and landowners jealously guarded their fishing rights against the periodic sorties of poachers.

While tenant farmers benefited most from the gentry's changing fortunes, the farm labourers who worked for them increasingly found the exhaustingly long hours of work and pitifully low wages intolerable, and by the turn of the century they were deserting the countryside in their thousands. Some journeyed in search of work to the cities of England, especially Liverpool, Manchester and London, or onwards even further to America, but the vast majority headed for the honey-pot of the industrial valleys of south Wales where jobs were plentiful and wages way in excess of any that could be obtained by working on the land. The gap between the standard of living which could be expected in the towns and that which was the lot of the majority in the countryside widened enormously at the turn of the century. Rural and urban Wales were growing inexorably apart.

A corn harvest near Llandeilo. D.C. Harries

THE BEAUTY OF SOUTH WALES

There is, perhaps, no tract of country in South Wales more beautiful than the Vale of Glamorgan.

It begins where the Rhymney river divides Monmouthshire from Glamorganshire; it ends where the Llwchwr forms the border stream of Cardiganshire, and stretches northward to the base of the mountain ranges that divide the Vale from those districts known as 'the hills'.

Travellers by the Great Western Railway pass through the whole length of the Vale, but they only get glimpses of the beautiful pasture-lands that fringe the Severn Sea. From Cardiff to Carmarthen the route taken by the railway is, in some places, very picturesque; but seaward of that line, where, as yet, the shrill whistle of the engine has not been heard, there are charming nooks and secluded places which, to the town-dweller, look like dreamland. The shoreline presents scenes of varied beauty, and the country around it is undulating rather than hilly, with glens and valleys sloping to the sea.

Marie Trevelyan, *Glimpses of Welsh Life and Character* (1893)

WELSH SQUIRES DESCRIBED

Let us take a glimpse of the Welsh squires of the present, of which there are three distinct classes. These are the political, the sporting, and the refined squire.

The first is a fussy, or excitable, though well-meaning man, whose sole object in life is to teach his tenants the political way they should go. He may be a Conservative or Liberal. . . . He is a man of his word, and above all things a firm adherent to the party and cause he espouses. . . .

The Welsh sporting squire is generally known as a 'happy-go-lucky' man, who is never in a more jovial mood than when the hounds are unkennelled, or he is in at the death. His whole heart is in sport, and he cares for little else. . . .

Early in the morning the sporting squire is ready for pleasure. When, during the hunting season . . . the hounds

George Barnes, head keeper of the Dinefwr (Dynevor) estate, Llandeilo, c. 1900. D.C. Harries

The empire bites back! Probably a scene of a sale at the winding-up of a small estate. D.C. Harries

are unkennelled, and every servant that can be spared attends his master to the meet, and soon the countryside rings with the sound of their voices.

In the shooting season the spaniels and other dogs are brought out, and the squire spends his morning in trying either the covers for pheasants or the stubble for partridges, and frequently by twelve o'clock he is able to return home with a well-filled bag. To him there is nothing more enjoyable than a long day on the moorlands that stretch to the sea, or a brilliant morning on the hill tops and slopes, when the sloes begin to turn from green to purple, and the soft autumnal haze creeps through the woodlands where golden and bronzed leaves fall among the scarlet berries of the wild rose, and the crimson bramble spray droop and trail on ferny hollows. . . .

The Welsh squire of the present, who is considered 'very refined', has been during a long minority looked after by trustees and guardians, who are determined that their ward shall be a perfect gentleman. . . . He likes a little – just a little sport; dislikes Wales, and above all things the Welsh language, which to his ultra-refined ear is a barbarous jargon composed of gutturals. When away from home he does not care to acknowledge his nationality, and while he remains in Wales he objects to its being thrust upon him. . . . This is the squire who goes yachting in the Mediterranean – takes trips to the

Hunting group, probably on the Dinefwr (Dynevor) estate, Llandeilo. D.C. Harries

Morris 'Baboon', a labourer from Llanrhaedr in north Wales.
John Thomas

The condition of the rural poor (nr Llandeilo), as highlighted by the
Royal Commission. D.C. Harries

'land of the midnight sun' – does a little tiger shooting in Africa – tries the mud-baths of New Zealand – has a 'Look' into the orange groves of Florida. . . .

Unlike his brothers the political and sporting squires, he has no friend among the people, and what is more, he does his utmost to avoid Wales and the Welsh, where from he draws all his money that carries him around the world. . . .

But, with a few exceptions, the old-timed hospitality of the past has ceased, and the manor houses that used to be 'open to all', are closed for ever. Rust, dust, and cobwebs cling to the closed portals of the once 'open house', where time has worked many changes.

A yawning chasm in many instances divides the Welsh squire of the present from the peasantry, and it may not be bridged.

Marie Trevelyan, *Glimpses of Welsh Life and Character* (1893)

Harvest home – haymaking. D.C. Harries

A LABOURER'S BUDGET IN THE BUILTH DISTRICT, MID-WALES, 1893

Edward Jones, farm labourer, wife and five children, wages 16*s*; extra harvest and job work 2*s*, equal to 18*s*.

Rent	1*s* 3*d*
Flour, 28 lb	3*s* 0*d*
Tea, ½ lb	0*s* 11*d*
Sugar, 6 lb	1*s* 3*d*
Bacon and lard	2*s* 2*d*
Potatoes	0*s* 2*d*
Milk	0*s* 3*d*
Coal	0*s* 10*d*
Wool (gratis)	————
Butter	2*s* 2*d*
Salt, pepper etc.	0*s* 1*d*
Soap	0*s* 4*d*
Club money	0*s* 6*d*
Clothing	3*s* 9*d*
Butcher's meat	1*s* 0*d*
Total	17*s* 8*d*

Royal Commission on Labour, The Agricultural Labourer, Vol. 11, Wales, 1893

THE MUSIC OF SCYTHES

Most of the farmer's life was spent in the field. . . . At the beginning of this century, the hay harvest was a communal effort and was governed by certain established rules. About a dozen farms combined for this purpose. The word 'combine' may mislead as it suggests a planned, arranged, effort. Nothing of the kind. These dozen or so farms had from time immemorial formed a workable group for this purpose. No meeting was called; no arrangements were made. Two farmers meeting at the approach of the season might possibly refer to the crop and the weather, but nothing

more. By an inherited rule one particular farm always led off, the others coming in their turn, and woe betide the man who disregarded the rule. They simply waited, therefore, for the leader to send his call for scyther or for machines. As a matter of fact, in the days of scythers, the hay harvest could not be carried out in any other way, for each farm needed at least nine or ten scythers. As a very small boy I well remember them on our fields – a row of them swinging their scythes lustily and rhythmically. In my ears there still rings the music of scythes. I have never heard it since. With the silence of the echoes in my ears it will vanish from the face of the earth for ever! Mowing machines came in rapidly at the beginning of this century and the scythes were hung up on the barn wall.

D. Parry Jones, *Welsh Country Upbringing* (1948)

THE COST OF HUNTING WITH HOUNDS

Last Saturday a large meeting of subscribers to the Pembrokeshire Hunt assembled at the Lion Hotel, Pembrokeshire, in response to a circular sent out by Mr C.W.R. Stokes, Hon. Secretary to the Hunt, to consider a letter received from Mr Lort Phillips, the popular master of the hunt, resigning the appointment.

Mr Vicherman said they met on a very melancholy occasion, to hear that they were going to lose the service of so good a master as Mr Lort Phillips. It appears that his ground of resignation is in consequence of the general depression which rendered it impossible to carry on the hounds with the present subscription, which he must say was a very inadequate one. From long experience he knew what an expense was entailed in keeping a pack of hounds, so well

Sewing class, Aberystwyth, c. 1890. Arthur Lewis

Domestic service, c. 1910. Arthur Lewis

attended to as the Pembrokeshire have been in every respect, for a miserable subscription of £1,000 a year, which subscription was only one half of the sum required. The general rule was that a pack of hounds hunting only one day a week cost £500 a year, and for a pack hunting four days a week there ought to be at least £2,000. That was what they subscribed in Essex for a four hour day a week pack. Although he deeply regretted Mr Lort Phillips's resignation, he was not surprised to hear that Mr Lort Phillips could not go on.

'The Mastership of the Pembrokeshire Hunt', *Tenby Observer*, 9 February 1893

GIRLS AT WORK

The attractions of farm life were said to be especially strong for young girls. Perhaps also town life has a greater fascination for them than for the men. The number of country girls . . . who go in for dressmaking is astounding, and one often wonders if half their number get any work at all. Welsh girls are also in great demand as domestic servants in England, owing to their character for industry, honesty, and cleanliness, partly (in many cases) of a bringing up on a small holding where a taste for work has been acquired. . . .

The watering and other tourist centres in North Wales are often the means of drawing good wages, a large amount of gratuities and presents from visitors, and what is sometimes more appreciated, a lively, albeit a hard time during the continuance of the short season. The best girls are almost invariably taken to England by the visitors and in time are the means of inducing others to follow in their wake.

Royal Commission on Labour, The Agricultural Labourer, Vol. 11, Wales, 1893

THE WELSH COUNTRYWOMAN

For the Welsh farm-wives there is no respite, and very often they have to do work which should be left to men. The women, as a rule, have a slight inclination to be parsimonious. Their object is not merely to lay by for the 'rainy day', but to leave something after them. To this end they will deny themselves many things. Others again save money for dress, and will wear very costly garments, but very subdued in colour.

Almost to a woman, Welsh farm-wives are very thrifty, scrupulously clean, and exceedingly industrious. When not engaged in household work, they devote their time to knitting, sewing, and repairing, and sometimes to patchwork, in which they generally are adept. The patchwork counterpanes are most neatly made, and quilted in fanciful designs.

It is singular to note how carefully these women endeavour to tread in the footprints of their mothers, and it appears to them almost sacrilege to turn any other way. There are exceptions to every rule, and some of the Welsh farm-wives are by no means paragons of perfection in any respect, but taking them as a whole they are very estimable.

These women never 'give up'; however indisposed they keep 'on their feet', and when once they take to their beds, it is an ominous token of approaching dissolution. Unless they live to a great age – which is frequently the case – they may be said to die in harness. It is very rare to meet with a Welsh farm-wife who is an invalid. As a rule they enjoy excellent health, and if delicate at all they invariably become rapidly consumptive. Great numbers of the Welsh farm-wives are the mothers of large families. Ten to twelve children is the average, but in many instances the number is fifteen, with occasionally a family of from eighteen to twenty children.

The women are very energetic, and can walk many miles without exhibiting the slightest symptoms of fatigue. There is an almost Spartan-like fortitude in their composition, and, as models of wifely fidelity, they are unsurpassed. I think I can

Milking. D.C. Harries

venture to state that separation and divorce are almost unknown among the farm-wives of the Vale of Glamorgan. The husbands may be unkind, dissolute, or lazy, but alike through evil report and good repute the wives will cling to them still. . . .

The cottage wives invariably enjoy excellent health – they have a supreme contempt for the doctor, and of some of them it can be said, to use their own expression, 'She carried all her teeth with her to the grave.' Although they avoid the doctor, except in extreme cases, they cling with tenacity of crabs to quackery and patent medicines. Quack doctors and medicine men are found in most rural districts, and the people's faith in them is often unbounded. They will take patent medicines in large quantities, and strange to say, they frequently double or treble the prescribed dose.

For herb infusions and similar concoctions they still cherish a secret and sincere love. Rosemary tea with treacle in it is one of their sovereign remedies for a cough; linseed tea, Spanish liquorice, butter and sugar or honey steeped in vinegar, are also much in request for the same purpose. For a cold, hot elderberry wine, treacle posset, egg flip, or 'gin hot', are recommended. The 'gin hot' of Wales is a stiff glass of Hamburg spirit or ordinary gin and beer heated to scalding point. This causes profuse perspiration. . . .

The cottage women always wear aprons of Welsh flannel, which are very large and comfortable. They are to be had in

A well-stocked farm in south Wales. D.C. Harries (detail)

grey and black, black and white, or a mingling of all. Over their shoulders in the winter time they wear small square flannel shawls, called 'turnovers' folded cornerwise, and printed rather low under the chin. On their heads they wear neat sun-bonnets of printed calico. . . . Welsh flannel dresses are still much worn, though they are being rapidly superseded by woollen and cotton fabrics of English manufacture.

Marie Trevelyan, *Glimpses of Welsh Life and Character* (1893)

A TASTE FOR LAVER

On many parts of the wild Welsh coast, women may be seen busily engaged in gathering laver, which is the sea liver-wort. . . . Great care has to be taken that the laver is free from sand, grit, and fine miniature winkles that sometimes cling to it. After a sufficient quantity has been gathered, the women wash the laver in the sea-water pools that abound on the shore. It is then taken home and washed and refreshed in fresh water, after which it is pressed very closely, until all the moisture is squeezed out. The cooking process is as follows:– A large saucepan is well rubbed with a piece of fat bacon, and a tablespoonful of liquid fat bacon is put in with a quantity of laver. The saucepan is then placed on a slow fire; a small folded towel is put on top of the laver, and the cover placed thereon. From time to time the laver is stirred until it is done, when it is taken out and chopped very finely. It is sold by the

pound, the price varying from sixpence to eightpence or tenpence. For cooking, it is forced into small round and flat cakes, about half an inch in thickness. These cakes are dipped in flour or oatmeal, and fried in boiling lard or bacon fat, and served very hot, as a rule with toasted bacon. . . . It is necessary to acquire a taste for laver, which if liked at all is generally liked very much. . . . The same women gather mussels and winkles, and in many instances samphire also.

Marie Trevelyan, *Glimpses of Welsh Life and Character* (1893)

BUTLER JAMES

We had a Welsh butler. Now, Welsh butlers are scarce. . . . I suppose 'buttling' does not appeal to the Cymric temperament, and consequently butlers . . . were, almost invariably imported across the border, or from the English-speaking parts of South Wales. But our James was a true Welshman as well as an excellent manservant. We children stood in wholesome awe of him, though he was generally good-natured – perhaps too good-natured – to us. For he used to help us in the taking of wasps' nests; and also he used to help us to 'sugar' at night for moths. All this was of course in James's milder moods, for he could be pretty severe with us on occasion, though I do not think he ever preached on any of our delinquencies. At the table he kept a sharp eye on our behaviour. 'Is it you or is it I, sir, who has to clean the silver?'

Miller and his wife, Llŷn Peninsula, c. 1904. J.G. Davies

A rural cottage on the Llŷn Peninsula, c. 1904. J.G. Davies

Probably a nanny working on a rural estate. D.C. Harries

he would whisper into our ears when we misused the spoons and forks; and often he emphasised this remark with a smart rap over our knuckles with the aforesaid piece of plate. . . .

A great joy it was to be called very early on some dark morning in the Christmas holidays, to eat breakfast by candlelight, and then to ride in the wan foggy atmosphere of the breaking dawn up to some moorland stretch, where a band of squires and farmers was collecting for a day's sport. . . . Almost as exciting was a big shoot of rabbits on Merlin's Hill, which adjoined the grounds of Bryn Myrddin. On these occasions we used to help the keeper and our elders by catching the wounded rabbits or by knocking them on the head with our sticks. Once a school-friend, a town-bred boy, stayed with me at Bryn Myrddin and participated with gusto in one of these rabbit drives. . . .

Herbert M. Vaughan, *The South Wales Squires* (1926)

HUNT BALLS AND MERRY DAYS

It was on the Tivyside Hunt that the social gaiety of the Tivyside gentry during the winter months mostly depended. There were large fields in those days of riders of every type, of mounts varying from blood horse to the humble jackass; many carriages attended the meets, and there was a fair sprinkling of followers on foot. The

Glanbrân mansion. D.C. Harries or Isaac Haley

country itself . . . was of the most sporting description. Deep wooded valleys, boggy stretches on the uplands and high banks, especially near the coast, to whose rocks Reynard often made for safety. In open weather too the many streams were swollen into torrents, and I remember seeing Mr Williams Brigstocke of Blaenpant being immersed in trying to cross the Cych when in flood. He disappeared entirely, horse, top-hat and all, in the muddy rushing water, and emerged on the further bank a sad spectacle.

The end of the season concluded with the Hunt Week and two public balls in the Guildhall at Cardigan, where about a hundred to a hundred and fifty members of the Hunt and their friends danced cheerily till well into the small hours of the morning. Hulley's string band from Swansea was the popular music of the day. Sometimes after supper the band broke out into song – 'The Jolly Coppersmith' being a special favourite, and of course the final gallop of 'John Peel'. Large parties were entertained at the country-houses for these balls, and for the Tivyside Races on the old Cilast course near Ffynone, which commands one of the finest views in West Wales. Those were merry days, and I am glad to think that I was old enough to enjoy them in the 'nineties.

Herbert M. Vaughan, *The South Wales Squires* (1926)

THE GYPSIES

There is a variety of names for these nomadic tribes in Wales, such as – the Family of Abram Wood; Egyptians; and the Family of Alabin, or Alabina. . . . Is there such a thing as a 'Welsh Gypsy', families living in the old primitive wild way? We know of a number of nomadic Gypsy families in Wales for scores of years who still travel, in a round, without leaving Welsh territory. . . . They are exceptionally artistic and skilful people; they are gold, lead and silver smiths, and excellent fiddle players and harpists. As fishermen they have no equals. Some of them live like gentry. . . . But there are also very poor families in their midst, begging from house to house; remembering that they are the people who customarily divine, or bewitch, and tell fortunes. They practise this gift in order to obtain sustenance and money; should they be refused what they request, they will threaten to bewitch you; other times they will tell your fortune for goods or for a particular sum of money . . . by now, education, the press, and the light cast by the great lantern of the Sunday School has starved all the Welsh wizards. . . . The Gypsy's most bountiful territory is the land of ignorance; and that is the reason why there have been only a few of them in Wales for years.

Pertheos, 'Y Sipsiwn Cymreig' ['The Welsh Gypsy'], *Cymru*, Vol. 20 (1901) (trans.)

Tinker and child, Llandovery district, c. 1910. D.C. Harries

Territorial march, Aberystwyth promenade, 1911. Arthur Lewis

ON MANOEUVRES

Early on Friday morning the combined forces of the Cheshire Brigade and Cardiganshire Battery moved out of camp and took part in a sham fight. Operations were conducted on the hillside in the vicinity of Capel Bangor. The operations, which were inspected by General Sir Francis Lloyd, were entered into with earnestness. On Saturday the Brigade was under the battalion commanders. Whilst returning to the camp on Friday a horse ridden by Major Mathias was injured and had to be destroyed on Saturday. On Thursday sports will be held and will include competition for officers and non-commissioned officers and men. On Monday the Cardiganshire Battery spent the day in riding drill and battery gun drill. The examinations for signallers also took place.

On Monday afternoon the Cheshire Territorials in camp at Lovesgrove marched through Aberystwyth and was a great attraction to visitors and town and country people. Coming down Penglais Hill, the men marched through North-gate-street, Queen's-road, and the Marine Terrace. Queen's-road was lined for a long distance on both sides by school children. The square on the Promenade at the entrance to Terrace-road was reserved for Col. Ommaney, the inspecting officer, the Mayor and Corporation with the Mayoress, Town Clerk, Colonel J.R. Howell, Mr George R. Pryse, Mr J. Ballinger and others. There were hundreds of spectators along the route, including many visitors from Stockport who cheered their friends and relatives when marching past. Headed by the regimental bands playing the marching past air 'Roy's Wife',

the troops proceeded through Pier-street, Great Dark gate-street, North-parade, when they had a five minute halt and then went without stopping through Llanbadarn back to camp. At the march past, the captain of each company saluted in review order and the men turned eyes right. The troops numbered nearly 5,000 and took ten minutes to pass the salute post. Contrary to the expectations of townspeople the Cardigan Battery who are in camp did not accompany the Brigade. . . .

The local Territorials have enjoyed their annual fortnight's training. . . . The majority of the Cheshires are strongly in favour of having the annual training again near Aberystwyth next year.

Cambrian News, 16 June 1911

LAUNCHING THE LIFEBOAT

Last Friday afternoon, the new lifeboat, the *John and Naomi Beattie* was launched in the presence of an immense crowd of visitors and residents. The weather was suitable for the occasion, a fair shy and rough sea with a stiff breeze which erected the waves with what poets call white horses. . . .

The lifeboat, which will replace the boat stationed at Aberystwyth by the Institution many years ago, was built by the Thames Ironworks company, is . . . thirty-five feet long by eight-and-a-half feet wide and rows ten oars, and is fitted with one drop keel and two water-ballast tanks. She is named the *John and Naomi Beattie*, as desired by Mrs Beattie of Clifton, who has generously presented the Institution with

Launch of the Aberystwyth lifeboat, 1906. Arthur Lewis

the cost of the new boat. The Royal National Lifeboat Institution has now 281 lifeboats under its management, thirty-four of which are stationed on the coast of Wales, and not a winter passes without some of the boats tendering good service in saving life from shipwreck.

Before the ceremony of launching at half past three o'clock, a procession was organised in Queens' road, where the lifeboat is housed. . . . After going through North parade, Great Dark-gate-street, down the Promenade, the procession returned to the Lifeboat Slip where a portion of the Promenade had been fenced off and a platform erected. The Mayor, receiving the boat said – Mr President, Lieut. Rowley, ladies and gentlemen . . . I have been out with the boat every time during the past twelve years and the local committee have approved of my action and presented me with a binocular glass. I have seen times when the boat could not get out beyond the Pier, when the oars were broken, and we could do nothing but let the boat drift. I am sure that the citizens of Aberystwyth will thank the Lifeboat Society for the boat and I will ask you to show your appreciation by giving three hearty cheers. (Cheers) The choir having sung 'To Those in Peril on the sea', the boat was then successfully launched, the battery of the Boys' Brigade firing Salutes, the choir singing the National Anthem, and the Band playing 'A Life on the Ocean Wave'.

Cambrian News, 17 August 1906

PHOTOGRAPHER CHARGED WITH CAMERA THEFT

Albert A. Hanlon, photographer, Liverpool, was charged with stealing a camera, with lens, and an album, value £8, the property of Messrs. Knipe and Culliford, Pier-Street. – Mr W.P. Owen solicitor, appeared for the prosecution. – Mr H.H. Knipe said that on July 29th last, the accused came to his shop and said he was a travelling photographer. He gave his name as Ashley Hansen – said he had been working for a while at Oswestry, having a wife and children at Berriew, Montgomeryshire. He had asked for work. From inquiries, witness had since found that statements made by prisoner were not correct.

Accused was ultimately engaged and was to go out with the camera, canvass for work, take orders, and receive money. He was not to go out of the town and immediate neighbourhood and was to return every night to develop what plates he had used during the day and also render an account of the orders and cash received. He was to receive a third part of the money as commission, witness supplying him with all necessary materials. Accused was to devote all his time to the work and did so for four or five days. A sum of 15s was advanced to him. He had taken certain orders. On July 6th, however, he disappeared, taking with him a complete camera, a specimen book containing twenty photographs, and lens which were witness's property. Witness did not see the articles from that date until last Thursday when accused was taken into custody, nor had he seen him until that morning.

Accused had taken a certain number of orders and witness had to complete them since. Prisoner had not brought a single penny to the shop and witness had applied for a warrant for his apprehension. . . . Witness pleaded 'guilty' and said of late he had been drifting from place to place. He asked for a chance to retrieve his past. – He was also charged with having embezzled the sums of 10s, 5s 6d, and 5s belonging to Messrs. Knipe and Culliford. . . .

The Bench committed him to three months' imprisonment on each case. – Mr Palmer hoped that after his six months he would try to lead a straightforward and honest life. – Mr Watkins said he was sorry that a man of so respected appearance should be in such a position. Accused: I appreciate your sympathy, gentlemen.

Cambrian News, 7 October 1904

Cardiganshire Constabulary Record Book, page for 1904

Montgomery Gaol, c. 1880. P.B. Abery

Wedding photograph, c. 1910. Slightly unusual for the time, as such photographs were more often taken in the studio.

WEDDING TRADITIONS

Curious wedding customs still prevail in Wales, especially in the western counties . . . although they are gradually declining in popular favour. Many of the young people now prefer going privately into the nearest town, and there getting married in a church, chapel, or before the registrar.

When a rural wedding takes place, the pathway or road leading from the bride's house to the church is previously carefully swept and sanded. Rushes and herbs are strewn all along the way, while here and there, bright coloured true lovers' knots are to be seen, and the aisle of the church is similarly decorated. As the bridal party return after the ceremony, they are 'chained', either with ordinary ropes, or ropes covered with flowers and evergreens, and the young couple shall not pass until the bridegroom pays toll.

Marie Trevelyan, *Glimpses of Welsh Life and Character* (1893)

UNSCRUPULOUS AGENTS AND UNREASONABLE LANDLORDS?

Agents are, also, too often bribed, and if the agent is not bribed the tenant or applicant for a farm may know the consequence. I am of the opinion that in many cases the agents are the cause of much of the oppression that is brought to bear upon the tenants. The landlords are often ignorant of the real state of affairs; they trust too implicitly to their agents, who naturally want to make as much profit out of the estate as possible.

[Evidence of Mr Lewis of Caeheulan, Penegoes.]

Yet English agents, who know more French than the tenant does English, who would be too vain and self-conscious even to stammer out a few French sentences in a drawing-room, lose patience with the Welshman if, in his distress, he refuses to carry on an unequal diplomatic or dialectical contest in the English language.

❖   ❖   ❖

We listened to the evidence of many Welsh witnesses as to arrangements made between them and agents, and we are convinced that in many cases the difficulty of language was at the root of the misunderstanding, and the parent of the quarrel between the parties.

❖   ❖   ❖

The landlord however, would not allow him to kill rabbits, but promised to do so himself, and to compensate for any loss sustained. In a short time the farm was covered with rabbits, which destroyed the crops, but he received no compensation, and no attempt was made to keep the game down.

❖   ❖   ❖

On the whole, we must come to the conclusion that the Welsh labourer has not as yet suffered from the agricultural depression with which the farmer has been so sorely stricken. Indeed, in one sense, the depression has indirectly improved his position. He has been able to obtain better terms and a more liberal treatment from the farmer, owing to the very fact that the latter is in difficulties and cannot afford to be so independent as formerly.

Report of the Royal Commission on Land in Wales and Monmouthshire, 1896

Shearing day, probably at Glanbrân, Carmarthenshire. D.C. Harries

William Morris Jones of the Home and Colonial Stores, Aberaeron.
D.C. Harries

An amazing range of meats on display at the local butcher.
D.C. Harries

Local forge, probably Carmarthenshire. D.C. Harries

SALTED MEAT AND BREAD

Mr David Davies, a labourer living in the parish of Llangybi, in Carnarvonshire, made the following statement as to the diet of the farmers in his neighbourhood.

The farmer's food is not of the best. It generally consists of salted meat, which is kept for a year or so until it is hard and difficult to eat. It is not often that the farmer's family or the servants get fresh meat, but when they do get it it is only the head of a cow or pig when one is killed. Generally when a cow is killed for the farmer's use it is one which could not be sold to a butcher. If a cow is a good one, it is always sold to pay the rent. The bread is better than it used to be, because they have failed to bake barley these last few years, and the farmers are compelled to buy wheaten bread. The butter is generally fresh and good, but the farmers can afford to give but very little to the servants, and little even to their own children.

Report of the Royal Commission on Land in Wales and Monmouthshire, 1896

BEGIN WITH PUDDING

In this latter county [Cardiganshire], in the days before the making of the railway connecting Aberystwyth with Shrewsbury and Oswestry, to be related of them, that it was their custom to begin dinner with the pudding, ever since one of them had chanced to die before reaching that course. The alleged change was supposed by a people who rarely tasted pudding to embody the rule of securing the best thing first.

Report of the Royal Commission on Land in Wales and Monmouthshire, 1896

WOOING AFTER DARK

The charges brought against Wales on the score of immorality are doubtless based to a certain extent on the survival in some agricultural districts of the old custom of night courtship, which is not peculiar to Wales, but occurs likewise among various European peoples as a survival from the life of the Middle Ages. It is frequently referred to in the poems of the 14th century

The Mountain Cottage Inn on the drovers' road near Lampeter. Better known as 'Tafarn Jem' after the licensee, Jemmah Davies, who stands in the picture. D.C. Harries

D. ap Gwilym, and it may be briefly described thus: the lover sallies forth at night and approaches the house where his fair one lives, he attracts her attention by gently tapping at her window. In some Welsh districts this is called *cnocio* or *streicio*, and in parts of Germany it is termed *fenstern*. . . . A similar practice is implied in several songs of Robert Burns. . . . At the window, as in the case of Romeo and Juliet, a conversation ensues which sometimes ends in the admission of the lover into the house, and in that case he and the young woman sit up together the greater part of the night. The charge of assuming a different position, for which the vocabulary of the English language provides the term *bundling* is usually denied and resented as a calumny.

Report of the Royal Commission on Land in Wales and Monmouthshire, 1896

RUNNING THE CHAPEL

The people in these Welsh villages have learnt during the last 150 years the most valuable lessons of self-government. Their chapels have been to them a splendid education in self-

government: they manage these chapels and manage their organisations with admirable skill and success.

Evidence of T.E. Ellis, Parliamentary Representative of the County of Merioneth. Report of the Royal Commission on Land in Wales and Monmouthshire, 1896

THE MOTHER TONGUE

The Code regulating public elementary schools now allows Welsh to be taught as a special subject, but it is doubtful whether Welsh will be very generally taken up. Such is the anxiety of Welsh parents to have their children taught English, and such is the reliance which they place on the Sunday School as a means of teaching the mother tongue. As a rule, however, the children in the country districts leave school before they have so far mastered English as to be able to make a free and comfortable use of it in conversation. Only a very small minority of them become really bilingual, as proved by their habitual use of Welsh for all purposes, domestic, social and religious. At most they retain perhaps

Rural industry (thought to be clog cutting), Carmarthenshire.
D.C. Harries

enough English learnt at school to be able to answer simple questions addressed to them in very plain terms. That they should shrink from giving evidence in English in courts of law is perfectly natural, as any Englishman possessed of a moderate acquaintance with French would at once comprehend, if he were called upon to undergo a cross-examination in that language.

Report of the Royal Commission on Land in Wales and Monmouthshire, 1896

A NEED FOR HOME COMFORTS AND ENTERTAINMENT

It is my firm conviction that the most serious and crying evil which farm labourers are subject to is the want of home comforts after their day's toil. Landlords ought to be compelled to provide servants' rooms which they can call their own and to which they could retire after their day's work to read or converse together, with a fire provided in the winter, and beds in a loft above. As it is, young men after supper at 7, have nowhere to go except to the stable loft, winter and summer, or the public-house, or stroll about and seek opportunities to disgrace young female servants. . . .

There are hardly any of the ordinary means of amusement, recreation, or of education available for the agricultural labourers. There has been hardly any effort to provide reading rooms or workmen's institutes in villages which are agricultural centres.

Royal Commission on Labour, The Agricultural Labourer, Wales, 1893

WORK OR THE WORKHOUSE

The family in question consists of husband and wife and eight children. Two of the children have just gone to service. The eldest girl, 18 years of age, is at home with indifferent health. Wages of husband £9 year with potato ground given by his employer, horse to cult and cart them, and to fetch coal twice a year.

> Rent £3 10s a year and rates 5s = £3 15s for a cottage and small garden.
> A pig is fed and sold.
> For flour, one sack every six weeks (30s to 33s).
> ¼ lb tea, from 1 lb to 2 lb sugar, butter-milk 2d to 3d a week, butter 2 lbs a week

After deducting the rent, the flour amounts to more than half the wages. No sweet milk is bought and no meat except 1 lb of bacon now and then. The different meals are as follows:

1) Breakfast, bread and milk
2) Dinner, potatoes and milk and sometimes bread and butter
3) Tea
4) Supper, porridge and milk. The milk in each instance is butter-milk.

The amount left for clothing does not exceed 1s 6d a week, but they pay their way and the children are clean and tidy and go to chapel every Sunday and oftener. They look fairly well but their constitutions will not stand treacle. . . . They cannot save money; were the husband to die, the workhouse must be their lot.

Evidence of Revd J. Owen, Royal Commission on Labour, The Agricultural Labourer, Wales, 1893

FROM DAWN TILL DARK

Here, as in other parts of Wales, servant girls appear to have the longest hours of all those engaged in farm service, extending from 5 a.m. until almost any hour of the night. Owing to want of system they are kept up very late. It was reported that they ought to be able to retire at 9 o'clock, but they hardly ever do so now.

Royal Commission on Labour, The Agricultural Labourer, Wales, 1893

TRAVEL

Over the centuries travelling across Wales had been severely hampered by the large mountain ranges running from north to south across the country and poor communications had been a key factor in frustrating the development of a sense of national unity. However, by the end of the nineteenth century this picture had been transformed by a communications revolution. Now Wales had one of the densest railway networks in the world, connecting all the major settlements and many of the lesser ones also, in the process making the country a cohesive unit in a way that had not been possible before. Nevertheless, the major rail communications were oriented from east to west, reflecting the reality of trade with England. Engineering feats such as the Severn Tunnel connecting south Wales and the west of England beneath the Bristol Channel, which was opened to much self-congratulation in 1888, underlined this reality. Elsewhere, industrial tramways and passenger trains snaked their way across moorland and vale, bridging rivers and steaming through mountain tunnels. One of the more picturesque journeys was that on the Snowdon Railway, constructed in 1896 to carry tourists to the peak of Wales's highest mountain. Although it became a popular attraction its reputation suffered an initial setback when the engine jumped the tracks on its maiden journey.

Extensive rail connections made mass tourism possible. Bathing towns such as Tenby, Aberystwyth and Swansea had attracted genteel visitors since the end of the eighteenth century, but the railway gave a new lease of life to these established resorts and enabled the creation of new ones. Along the north Wales coast Rhyl, Prestatyn and Llandudno increasingly served the holidaying workers of Lancashire, while in south Wales, Barry Island became the favoured destination for day-tripping miners and their families. In mid-Wales the spa towns of Llandrindod Wells and Llangamarch Wells enjoyed a brief high-noon as middle-class travellers sought relief from the stresses and strains of everyday life — one incongruous figure in their midst was the German Kaiser.

As well as better rail communications, wider use of the bicycle afforded the ordinary traveller much greater personal freedom and mobility than ever before, while the advent of motorised travel created new possibilities for the more well-to-do. These innovations imparted a new thrill of speed which often frightened onlookers, even to the extent of the police making arrests for riding a bicycle 'furiously'! Small numbers of collisions and mishaps were an early indication that roads were to become more dangerous places for both pedestrian and traveller in the twentieth century.

The engine The Prince of Wales *on the Vale of Rheidol Railway, 1915. Arthur Lewis*

THE ARRIVAL OF THE INTERNAL COMBUSTION ENGINE

There were two or three motorcycles in the town by 1906. The pioneer, a Scott, belonged to J.R. Morgan the headmaster of the county School; it drew a side-car oddly shaped like a bath chair. He also rode a high Dursley-Pederson cycle with hammock saddle and cantilever frame, a masterpiece of engineering if not of comfort. Another local motorcycle, a light weight French Motors acoche, made a noise like a sewing machine: those were the days of experiment in cycles and motorcars. The motorcar arrived slowly. The first was a high-bodied French car belonging to Partridge a bank manager; crowds gathered on Saturday afternoon in 1905 to see him drive off in a cloud of smoke after repeated starts. The next two were the large Daimlers of the company's General Manager, which arrived by rail in 1907. The other three belonged to a doctor, a hotel proprietor and an engineer.

Arthur Gray-Jones, *A History of Ebbw Vale* (1970)

THE RAILWAY TRADE

I do not know of any district which, while still remaining purely agricultural, has been so greatly influenced by the introduction of railways as this portion of Anglesey. It has enabled the poorer classes to make large sums of money out of commodities which in other districts are generally neglected, and it has also enabled them to spend such money freely upon excursions and other forms of pleasure previously unknown to them.

Royal Commission on Labour, The Agricultural Labourer, Wales, 1893

SNOWDON TRAIN JUMPS ITS TRACKS

The Snowdon railway was officially opened on Saturday and Sunday. A small number of people from Llandudno and other places ascended the mountain in the train on Saturday, despite the cold and the fog. This morning, a large crowd from Caernarfon and elsewhere came to Llanberis to spend the day, and about fifty-five of them travelled on the new line. It was a freezing morning and the mountain was under cloud, but it was dry and promising. The sky cleared, and the sun appeared to revive the area in the afternoon. The train had a safe journey until it reached the mountain's shoulder – a narrow spot with two steep precipices of hundreds of yards, called Crib Goch. It was at this point that the engine went out of control, because of the pressure on it. It jumped the rails, roaring headlong down the mountain on the Nant Uchaf side.

The engineer and fireman escaped by jumping off the engine, and in their fright at seeing the carriages begin to run back down the line, two passengers jumped out – Mr Ellis Roberts of the Padarn Villa Hotel, Llanberis, and a gentleman from Oswestry. Mr Roberts broke his leg, and the

Believed to be a 1915 2¼ hp James on a Carmarthenshire byroad.

The Snowdon Mountain Railway – before the fateful crash in 1896 (above) and the engine immediately after the disaster (below)

other injured his head. Because the other passengers kept their heads and retained self-control, not one of them was hurt.

Needless to say that the accident has aroused fear, and attracted great attention. This morning (Tuesday) Mr E. Roberts died from his injuries.

Baner ac Amserau Cymru, 8 April 1896 (trans.)

JOURNEY TO THE TOP

Since its opening in 1896 this railway has enabled thousands of visitors to reach the summit of Snowdon, the highest mountain in England or Wales. Built on the system in use on the Alpine Railways, the line is the only one of its kind in the British Isles. . . .

Visitors who arrive at Llanberis by the London and North Western Railway have no difficulty in finding the pretty terminus of the Rack Railway, built in Swiss chalet style, and fitted with the usual equipment of a modern railway station, including first class refreshment and tea-rooms. On the western side of the summit the terminus is soon reached, and 20 paces on the left of the platform the traveller attains the

very peak of the cairn. For the sake of the magnificent spectacle, many visitors spend the night at the hotel on the Snowdon summit in order that they may view the sun rising over the mountain.

'Snowdon Mountain Rack Railway', *The Railway Magazine*, Vol. 33 (1913)

The Ammanford–Llandeilo omnibus after crashing into the ramparts of Llandeilo bridge, c. 1911. D.C. Harries

FIRST HORSELESS CARRIAGE ACCIDENT

The advent of the motor car into Wales has been signalised by an unfortunate accident. One of the Thorneycroft's horseless carriages – the first of its class we believe built in England – has been purchased by the South Wales Motor Car and Cycle Company for the purpose of conveying ship's stores and other merchandise from Cardiff to Barry Docks, and it has been duly brought by road from London.

When it had crossed the brawling Rumney River from Newport on Saturday, this motor car was the first to have got into the confines of the Principality. The car left Newport about 11 o'clock with a party of eight on board, including the driver. The appearance of the horseless carriage produced, of course, a keen curiosity and speculation amongst the citizens of the villages passed through on route, especially at St. Mellons, where a halt was called for refreshments.

After a few minutes the journey was resumed and all went well until the eastern entrance to the borough was reached. When the Royal Oak Hotel had been passed, Mr William Duncan, secretary of the company, alighted, from the rear of the vehicle, lost his footing, and essayed to remount in front while the engine was in motion. The iron step seems to have been greasy from mud upon it and Mr Duncan slipped. He fell to the ground with his left foot right in the line of the advancing car, and before it could be stopped Mr Duncan

had his foot crushed to a pulp. He was picked up and taken by the horseless carriage to the Infirmary, Cardiff which was fortunately close at hand, and it was found necessary to cut away parts of the maimed member.

The motor car was brought through Cardiff, where the novelty evoked only passing notice until it was temporarily pulled up in front of the Royal Hotel. Here a considerable crowd speedily gathered, obstructing the side walk, and in view of this circumstance the vehicle was soon taken away.

South Wales Echo, 2 January 1897

YOUNG WOMAN KILLED BY OVERTURNED MOTOR CAR

On Tuesday night about eleven o'clock a motor car driven by Edward Gwynne Parry of 42, The Drive, Woodstock Avenue, Hendon, London, who is a son of Dr Parry, Pontycymmer, the other occupants being Mr Thomas Jenkins, steel merchant, Porth, Glam., Miss Annie Patterson and Miss Florence Gertrude Patterson, whose father resides at 2, Portland Road, Aberystwyth, were proceeding from Aberystwyth to New Quay. At the right angle turn in the road near Henfynyw Church the driver apparently failed to negotiate the car at this very dangerous curve. The car was upset in the well-known pool of mud and water on the left hand side in proceeding to Ffosffin. All the occupants were pinned underneath the car, and were all immersed in the water, which after rains may be three feet deep. Fortunately for them, Mr T.I. Enoch of Abermarles was just then driving home in his car and was on the spot in a few minutes. With the assistance of Mr Rhys Evans, Ffosffin cross, they were able to release three of the occupants without injury but the young woman Florence was found to be dead.

The body of the dead woman was taken to the Red Lion Inn, Ffosffin, where it lies awaiting an inquest. The other occupants of the car went to Aberayron.

The deceased girl who was seventeen years of age was formerly a pupil at Aberystwyth County School and was now in service to Miss Fuller, Penglaise Road. Her sister, who is twenty-one years of age, was on a visit from Manchester where she had been employed. Both were well known in Aberystwyth where the news of the accident was received with great sorrow, and the deepest sympathy is extended to the father who is a gardener.

Cambrian News, 16 May 1913

STRIKE HALTS TRAINS

The stoppage of through trains on the Cambrian and G.W.R. railways out of Aberystwyth put business people and visitors on Friday to great inconvenience. The Post Office was crowded with visitors sending telegrams to their friends and the Railway Station was besieged by people asking questions to which no reliable answers could be given. Mr Thomas, the courtroom stationmaster and the other officials readily gave

Attempt to stop the Great Western bus at Aberystwyth during the 1911 railway strike. Arthur Lewis

Jones Brothers' charabanc near Aberystwyth in 1910. Arthur Lewis

all the information they possessed to questions. . . . The Cambrian Company issued a circular giving notice that, owing to the labour difficulty, the company could not undertake to maintain the advertised service of passenger trains, but trains would be run as might be practicable. . . . On Saturday morning the strikers marched to the engine sheds through the goods yard and persuaded those who were working to cease work. There was, however, a 'truce' for the arrival of the morning mail which came in two sections without interference. Hundreds of visitors had congregated at the Railway Station to go away by the eight o'clock train which was merged in the 8.10, but was not supposed to go further than Welshpool. Carriages waiting at the platform for an engine were filled, but no engine was allowed to be used. An announcement was made that the train would not run and that no train would depart or arrive until further notice, resulting in a dislocation of business which people hardly believed to have been possible. It was like a stroke of paralysis. The only services from Aberystwyth were the round motor to New Quay, and Aberayron, and trains on the Vale of Rheidol Railway. On the Cambrian and Great Western, engine fires were extinguished and the signal boxes locked up.

Poster giving notice of the Cambrian Railways strike of 1911.
Arthur Lewis

❖ ❖ ❖

People have been astounded that railway trains were not running, that telegrams were not sent, that letters were not received, and that parcels were not delivered. They said that they had never heard of such a state of things. This was quite true, but those who had given the subject thought had realised the possibility long ago, and now it has been made clear that railway companies can be held up, as they have been held up since Thursday, the 17th, until Sunday, the 20th, it is clear that something will have to be done by the State to make a recurrence of the evil in the future absolutely impossible. There is in our opinion, only one effective remedy, and that is the nationalisation of railways. We have urged railway nationalisation, as our readers know, not so much as a means of dealing with the sort of thing that has now arisen, but as a means of increasing the national prosperity of the securing for the whole country the same equalness of treatment as is secured by the postal service, the telegram service, and the parcel post service. We believe the railway companies are as much to blame as anybody for the deadlock which arose and whether the trouble was ended in a day or two or was continued for six months is of comparative little importance. There is the fact that the country can be deprived of food, commercial commodities, letters, telegrams, and means of transit. This state of things, deplorable in its disastrous consequences, would have been impossible if all the railways in the country had been in the hands of the State.

Cambrian News, 25 August 1911

THE PENNY-FARTHING

I bought a 'Penny-farthing' bicycle – the big wheel was about 6 ft high and the little wheel was about 2 ft in circumference, fitted to a 'Backbone'. After some help from a friend I managed to leap up to the high saddle and ride to and from work for 3½ miles of rough road. There were no steam rollers in those days and the 3½ miles home in the evenings if the weather was fine was most enjoyable, you could see over the hedge rows, but if you had a spill you had a very long way to fall. I fortunately escaped accident.

Francis Hughes (b. 1873), 'I remember . . .' (Cardiff Library Archive, Qo L: 8-94: 656.21)

CARDIFF CORPORATION TRAMWAYS, *RULES AND REGULATIONS FOR DRIVERS AND CONDUCTORS* (1905)

Rules for Drivers and Conductors

2. Conductors and drivers must be civil and obliging to the public, and to answer politely and respectfully any inquiry that may be made by passengers. Avoid arguments with passengers, and give badge numbers and names when asked for. . . .

Penny-farthing outside the studio of T.T. Mathias

render every assistance. The absence of a report from Drivers and Conductors as to any accident in which they are concerned will result in dismissal. . . .

24. Drivers and Conductors reported for entering public-houses whilst in uniform, or drinking intoxicating liquor while on duty, will be summarily dismissed.

25. Smoking whilst on duty is strictly prohibited. Drivers and Conductors are forbidden to eat their meals on the car.

Running Rules

3. Drivers must not exceed two miles per hour when running through frogs and overhead line crossings, and round all curves, and must shut off current while passing section insulators, and also when running under frogs where practicable. If the trolley leaves the line the conductor must at once signal to the driver who must turn the controller to the off position, and instantly stop the car. . . .

6. The foot gong must always be used to clear traffic, and before crossing and at the junction of intersecting streets, and when passing a car either running or setting down passengers. . . .

25. Drivers must sound the gong and apply the brake when approaching a vehicle on the track, so as to give sufficient room for it to get out of the way if the wheels should slide, and when following vehicles to allow ample space that in the event of the former pulling up suddenly no collision may result therefrom.

Note – Drivers will be held responsible for damage caused by inattention or careless driving.

10. Drivers and Conductors must take a written report of all cases of cars being **three or more** minutes late, or out of place, giving a reason, particular care must be taken in reporting all cases of delay or obstruction. Also two cars meeting on a single line must be reported. **In all such cases the driver of the car nearest a loop must turn back**.

11. Drivers and Conductors must not allow a person without proper authority or permission to take their cars and work them any journey or part of journey, and are prohibited from allowing a substitute to perform their duties and from exchanging duty with other servants, without permission. No person without special authority must be allowed to ride on either platform. . . .

15. Drivers and Conductors must be reported in writing, immediately on being relieved from duty, whenever an accident of any nature (however trivial) happens to or is caused by their car, or any accident to which they may be witnesses, whereby any vehicle belonging to outside parties is damaged, or persons injured, no matter how slightly, whether by falling when getting off, or in any other manner. Stop the car at once and ascertain the extent of damage or injury done, and (no matter who may be to blame for the occurrence) obtain the names and addresses of the persons injured or causing the damage, and the names in full and addresses or place of business of persons witness to the occurrence. In cases of personal injury show sympathy and

Swansea, the street complete with the city trams in 1893.
Francis Frith & Co.

Getting to the church on time, c. 1910. D.C. Harries

THE RAILWAY COMES TO ABERAERON

A glance at the railway map of England and Wales produces the impression that there are now very few districts which are not in some way served by one or more railways. And yet, in many counties, there are still numerous villages, and even good-sized towns, which are so far removed from a railway that the majority of their inhabitants rarely if ever travel by rail, the difficulty of getting to and from the nearest station presenting a barrier which only those who must travel, or who are able to afford the expenditure of time and money which every journey involves, can surmount. This is particularly so in western counties of Wales, where many districts are so remote from the railway that they have perforce remained undeveloped solely owing to lack of transport facilities.

The opening, in 1911, of the railway to Aberayron, a town by no means unimportant on the shores of Cardigan Bay, marked the completion of an undertaking which has for the last 30 years been in progress. Many attempts had been made to place Aberayron in direct rail communication with the outer world, but all were doomed to failure, and only the persistent efforts of a small body of public-spirited men . . . brought the project through many vicissitudes to a successful issue. . . .

Train services are provided between Lampeter and Aberayron by means of a rail auto-car, one class only. . . . Every day there are four trains in each direction, the 12 miles between Lampeter and Aberayron being covered in about 50 minutes. Through connections are established with the 9.15 p.m., 1 a.m., 8.45 a.m., and 11.30 a.m. from Paddington.

Alfred W. Arthurton, 'The Lampeter and Aberayron Railway', *The Railway Magazine*, Vol. 34 (1914)

'A WARNING TO CYCLISTS'

At the Pontypridd police-court on Wednesday a respectably dressed young man named Evan Lewis was summoned for riding a bike furiously.

P.C. James stated that ten past six on Saturday week he saw defendant riding a bicycle at a furious rate from the direction of the Tumble. He called out to him and told him to ride steadier. Defendant turned into Mill-street and ran into a man. Witness told him he would have to report him. Later in the evening he saw the officer and told him that he lost control over the machine. He was riding at the rate of 15 miles an hour. . . .

Defendant was fined 5*s*.

Pontypridd Observer, 30 April 1898

UNDER THE RIVER SEVERN

The Severn Tunnel was opened for goods traffic on the 1st September, 1886, on which date a service consisting of nine goods and mineral trains in each direction was inaugurated. These trains, however, were not the very first trains carrying traffic which passed through the Tunnel, as, for the purpose of demonstrating the capabilities of the new route, an experimental trip had been run on the ninth of the previous January, with a train of wagons containing coal from Aberdare destined for shipment at Southampton. The remarkable feature of this trip was that the coal was worked and raised to the surface in the morning, loaded into the wagons, weighed, invoiced and running via the Severn Tunnel, Bristol and Salisbury, deposited alongside the ship, at Southampton, ready for tipping into the hold, the same evening. . . .

On the 1st December, 1886, passenger trains for the first time ran through the Tunnel, the first train being that which left Bristol at 6.15 a.m. and arrived at Cardiff at 7.45 a.m. . . . on the 1st July, 1889, through trains between London on the one hand and South Wales, on the other, commenced to run: and at the present time passengers service consists of eleven local trams in each direction, and six 'down' and 'up' through trams, making a total of thirty-three trams during the day. . . .

The average time occupied by a passenger train running through the Tunnel is seven minutes and by goods train twenty minutes.

Thomas A. Walker, *The Severn Tunnel* (1888)

Jubilation at the opening of the Aberaeron Railway in 1911. Arthur Lewis

The 'Rheidol', originally destined for the cane fields of Brazil, finding work on the Vale of Rheidol line, c. 1910. Arthur Lewis

Llandovery station on the London and North Western Line, c. 1910. D.C. Harries

Road building, Carmarthenshire. D.C. Harries

Steam traction lorry owned by William Jeffrys of Llandeilo. D.C. Harries

THE POST OFFICE

Letters

For letters not over 4 oz, 1*d*. For every additional 2 oz, ½*d*. Double payment is called for every letter without a stamp.

Books

Books not exceeding 2 oz, ½*d*, ½*d* for each 2 oz above this.

Newspapers

For each newspaper ½*d*, but if two or more are posted together they are charged as for books, namely ½*d* per 2 oz.

Post Cards

A message can be sent by postcard, which can be purchased for 7*d* or 8*d* a dozen – the address on one side and the note on the other. A plain card can be used with a ½*d* stamp.

Parcels

Parcels can be sent through the post at the following rates:–

Not over 1 pound					3*d*
Over 1 pound and under 2 pounds					4*d*
"	2 pounds	"	3 pounds		5*d*
"	3	"	"	4 "	6*d*
"	4	"	"	5 "	7*d*
"	5	"	"	6 "	8*d*
"	6	"	"	7 "	9*d*
"	7	"	"	8 "	10*d*
"	8	"	"	9 "	11*d*
"	9	"	"	11 "	1*s*

No parcel over 11 lb can be sent through the post. Parcels measuring over 3 feet 6 inches cannot be sent.

Registered Letters

For a payment of 2 pence in addition to the carriage, it is possible to register any letter or parcel. This payment secures compensation for lost or damaged post up to £5. No one should send a letter containing money or valuables, without first registering them. No compensation can be paid if registered envelopes, available at post offices, are not used.

Almanac Caergybi, 1904 (trans.)

WAITING FOR THE POST

My Dear Elin,

I felt very disappointed when I came from chapel to my room this morning. I had convinced myself that there would be a letter from you waiting for me with the breakfast dishes, and I wondered what it would contain while the people were half reciting, half singing the one hundred and nineteenth psalm. I ran up the stairs to my room, – there was nothing from you. I sat in front of the fire with my head in my hands, and I said, – 'Damn it! she forgot all about me as soon as she got well; I wish she were still ill. . . .'

But as I read through the other letters, the porter knocked on the door again, – 'Parcel Post, sir'. For a moment I thought it was a pack of books I was expecting . . . but soon I saw your handwriting, – and I would recognise it among thousands, – and in a moment I was in the best temper ever. . . . I am writing in thanks for your present, as you see, by return of post. . . .

Loving wishes, Owen.

Owen M. Edwards to Ellen Edwards, 25 February 1890 (trans.)

Cynghordy post office at the turn of the century.
D.C. Harries

The Llanwrtyd coach 'Benjamin Jones' carrying passengers and mail, c. 1905. D.C. Harries

The brake 'General Buller' taking visitors to wonder at the picturesque falls and bridges at Devil's Bridge, c. 1910. Arthur Lewis

New railway through the Upper Afan Valley, 1898

Dog cart. D.C. Harries

Daily life pauses at Pen-bont Rhydybeddau. Arthur Lewis

Chapter 5

CULTURE AND RELIGION

Cultural life in Wales in the late nineteenth century was heavily influenced by the Nonconformist chapels, even in ostensibly secular activities such as choral singing. During the nineteenth century Nonconformity had developed into a quintessentially working-class religion in Wales and the chapels and their ministers had assumed the mantle of tribunes of the people. Welsh in their language and democratic in their ethos, the different denominations were united by their dogged struggle against the privileges and power of the predominantly Anglicised and Conservative Church of England.

When the religious revival of 1904/5 broke under the inspired leadership of Evan Roberts it appealed especially to women and young people, two groups which were marginalised by organised religion, whatever its hue. The revival was a great outpouring of emotion during which thousands flocked back to the chapels and turned their backs on 'ungodly' activities such as rugby football. In fact, the newspapers reported Evan Roberts's prayer meetings much as they would have written about a rugby match. However, the revival proved to be short-lived in its effects. Rather than representing a resurgence of religion, the revival was the last rage against Nonconformity's dying light.

Even though only half the people spoke Welsh by 1900, the language continued to sustain a vibrant culture in these decades. Indeed, there was a cultural renaissance as young poets, novelists and scholars flexed their literary muscles and a steady stream of books flowed from the presses. This renaissance was due in part to the products of the state-funded County Schools after 1889 and the existence of the three colleges of the federal University of Wales. The University provided a sound scholarly basis for the study of Welsh history and literature. Welsh-language newspapers, periodicals and books continued to thrive, and the annual National Eisteddfod remained the country's most popular cultural festival, alternating between locations in north and south Wales every other year and attracting visitors in their thousands. It encompassed a wider range of cultural activities, although literary and musical competitions attracted the greatest interest and attention. Success in an eisteddfodic contest was an esteemed and coveted achievement.

Side by side with this established cultural activity was the beginnings of an emerging English-language culture. Writers such as Howard Spring and Joseph Keating sowed the seeds of a new Anglo-Welsh literature which would flourish between the wars. Without doubt the most controversial of the new writers was the pugnacious Caradoc Evans whose depictions of rural life as a brutalising experience, in which adherents of the Nonconformist chapels were complicit, challenged the self-image of the champions of Nonconformist rural life who clearly thought of themselves in terms of a cultured haven cocooned from the worst elements of modern life. His views did not go unchallenged.

Pwllheli Session, 1904. J.G. Davies

Deunant school, girls class (above) and boys class (below), 1904. J.G. Davies

A LANGUAGE IN DANGER

Our language is today in enormous danger. An authority no less than Professor Zimmer of Berlin has called attention to the fact that the whole movement to obtain 'higher education', which has such a grip in Wales today, is organised on foreign lines, and not on national ones. It depends upon the present age whether Wales will remain a nation or whether she is sucked into England and swept from the world's view after two thousand years of history! There cannot be two national languages in any country; in the end one must displace the other. It is necessary to do as did countries on the Continent decades ago and call for the Welsh language in every school in Wales. If public opinion can be strengthened on this subject, then it will be easy to achieve it. Hungary made its language compulsory in the schools in 1844, Bohemia in 1860, and Bulgaria in 1800, and they were all subject peoples. We have not yet, in the twentieth century, made the Welsh language so, even though the number of foreign immigrants to Wales was greater during the last thirty years than ever before. In other countries the foreign element is sucked into the national body through the medium of the schools. Had our leaders battled to make the Welsh language compulsory when Forster's Education Act (1870) was passed, we would today be a Welsh nation from Holyhead to Cardiff, and the Welsh language would be a protection against the English flood. A language can only hold its ground in a country where 55 per cent use it. What is the state of some of our counties? In Glamorgan Welsh is used by 35 per cent; Pembroke, 34 per cent; Monmouth, 13 per cent; Radnor, 6 per cent. This shows that our language is in enormous danger. Cultivating public opinion ought to be the principal aim of branches of the Cymmrodorion Society. Also, we must give more support to the national press if we are serious in our work of building a nation. At present, for every shilling we spend on Welsh books and periodicals, we spend pounds on English ones. This practice must be turned around. Build the nation on the Celtic lines which are your own heritage, so that Wales can develop itself to enable it to contribute its own special share to the world's thought and art. Only through the language can this be done. Here is work for the aristocracy and the people to partake in. No man can hold back and retain his honour.

'Cymru a'r Gymraeg [Wales and the Welsh Language]', *Y Gymraes*, Vol. XVII (1913) (trans.)

PUNISHED FOR SPEAKING WELSH

Quickly the word went round that a new boy, and simple too, had come to school. The eyes of a number of cruel children were on me – I knew the lot of them, loud-mouthed children from the village for the most part – they are still no better. The teacher had told me quietly not to speak a word of Welsh; but those bad lads did everything they could to make me shout, and at last they succeeded. I lost my temper and I began to speak my mind to the treacherous cur who was scheming how to torment me. As soon as I uttered

Students at the Bangor Normal College at the turn of the century. The Normal colleges were established to train teachers, especially for staffing elementary schools.

my broad Welsh, everyone laughed and a string was put about my neck with a heavy wooden token attached to it. I didn't know what on earth it was; I had seen a similar device around the neck of a dog to prevent its running after sheep. . . . I understood thereafter that it was for speaking Welsh that it was hung around one's neck. That token hung about my neck hundreds of times afterwards. . . .

It has been a consolation to me until today that I never attempted to have peace from the token by transferring it to someone else. I knew nothing of the principle of the thing, but my nature rebelled against the accursed manner of destroying the bases of a child's character. Teaching a child to watch out for a smaller child speaking his mother tongue in order to transfer the punishment to him! No, the token never left my neck, I suffered a caning everyday as the end of school arrived.

Owen M. Edwards, *Clych Atgof* (1921) (trans.)

CONDUCTING A CENSUS

If persons speak only Welsh how are they expected to fill in their papers in English? Common sense would at once reply, 'Supply them with Census papers printed in Welsh'. This was intended to be done, and a quantity of such papers printed entirely in Welsh have been prepared for that purpose, but here again officialdom has blundered, and, presumably to save trouble, some purely Welsh districts have only been supplied with 5 per cent of the Welsh papers, the other 95 per cent being entirely in English! This only needs to be known to be condemned. In the case of Cardiff, I am told that not a single Welsh paper has been received by enumerators for distribution. As a matter of principle, and in order to test the question of a Welsh householder's right to demand a Welsh census paper, I today declined to take in the English census paper offered me by the enumerator for this district.

Beriah Gwynfe Evans on the Census of 1891, *South Wales Daily News*, 2 April 1891

Bethania Sunday School (Cardigan?) towards the end of the 1890s

LEARNING WELSH BY THE BIBLE

The work of the Sunday School covers the whole extent to which the bulk of the Welsh people are taught Welsh at all outside their hearths and homes; for the public elementary schools have till lately been almost wholly devoted, so far as language is concerned, to the teaching of English, and the great majority of them continue so, though the Code now recognises Welsh as an optional and special subject. Looking at the Sunday-school teaching of Welsh as a whole, one may say that the edifice is in a manner made complete by the role played by literary societies, and literary competitions in which prizes are given for singing, for writing Welsh, both prose and verse, and, for translating from English into Welsh, and vice versa. These competitions do not occur more than once a year even in the neighbourhoods where they are the rule; and, speaking generally, they are sporadic and dependent for their origination on individuals who feel interested in Welsh and Welsh music. They are altogether a very indefinite quantity, but literary societies have been of late becoming more general and somewhat more permanent. They all serve, however, as feeders to the Eisteddfod, and they have in recent years exercised great influence on the cultivation of Welsh and Welsh literature. It is needless to remark that, so far as regards Welsh prose, the style of the authorised version of the

Welsh Bible is the ideal of those who try to write and speak good Welsh. The fact that the Bible forms the earliest prose reading of the youth of Wales, and that they commit a great deal to memory under the direction of the Sunday School, makes that result unavoidable . . . this literary or standard Welsh is practically a dialect to itself, distinct from the colloquial language consisting of the dialects. . . .

Unfortunately this position of supremacy of literary Welsh is now more and more contested by the shoddy Welsh which prevails in many of the newspapers published in Welsh.

Report of the Royal Commission on Land in Wales and Monmouthshire, 1896

CHAPEL VERSUS CHURCH

The spiritual wants of the Welsh people are attended to by Nonconformity. The Nonconformist chapels are crowded, but the churches of the Establishment are forsaken in every rural district in Wales. It is the same old story – it is not the people who do the work who receive the pay. In fact, it is a *very* old story.

David Lloyd George, speech to the Liberation Society, 1890

Capel Als, an important Nonconformist chapel in Llanelli, 1896. Francis Frith & Co

METHODIST FIRST: WELSHMAN SECOND

There was a large choice: Ebenezer, Zion, Penuel, Tabernacle, Goshen, Brynhyfryd, Moriah, Jerusalem. This list omits the Anglican and Roman Catholic churches and the English nonconformist churches. We had besides, a small room-full of Latter Day Saints, and two or three who dabbled in Spiritualism and went to secret seances. A mesmerist who came amongst us with his black art was publicly mobbed. My choice in fact was pre-determined by my Calvinistic ancestry. My great-grandfather, grandfather, his brother, and my own father were deacons of the Welsh Calvinistic Methodist or Presbyterian Church. . . .

I felt and knew myself to be a Methodist much more actively and intensely than I felt myself to be a Welshman. . . . I have been much more shaped by the Wales of the Preachers than by the Wales of the Princes or the Wales of the Politicians.

The sermons of the great Welsh preachers are full of picture-thinking and it is an incomparable medium for reaching the multitude. Mr Lloyd George has used this gift and anyone who has analysed a popular speech by him has found it to be a series of pictures and metaphors. Pulpit imagery varied in artistic quality. . . .

The next instruments of my theological education were the Sunday School and the Children's Meeting. . . .

In the Children's Meeting the method was that of the catechism. . . . Our conductor was a man with a shake and shiver in his voice and his tremulous tearful style had an immense effect on the children, and we answered together in an ever swelling chorus . . . in Welsh. . . .

The minute study of the Scriptures was fostered by a system of graded Sunday School examinations and the publication annually of the commentaries by divines belonging to the denomination. I sat the first of these, open to the country, in 1884, and came out seventh out of sixty-seven with my name printed in the *Amserau* (*Times*), an unforgettable milestone. I kept the cutting for years. I finished in 1890 by being bracketed first for the Gold Medal, open to all members of the denomination, an achievement which gave my father and mother more pleasure than anything else I ever did.

Thomas Jones, *Rhymney Memories* (1938)

'WALK ON TIPTOE IN THE HOUSE OF GOD!'

In those days, in my earliest days, the chapel played a highly important part in the lives of all the people of the valley. Soon it was to lose its supremacy; but I was in time to know it before its light deepened into a twilight which, except for an occasional flicker and one big burst of lightning at the Welsh revival, has not brightened much since.

Saron Chapel, a congregational chapel, was big; indeed, older people boasted that it was the biggest in the valley, and it probably was. You entered by going down a step or two into a porch, where could be read secular Parish notices about the Rates as well as sacred information about chapel functions like the Band of Hope and other chapel meetings.

The interior of Saron was very much like the interior of other chapels except that Saron was bigger – oblong and without any gaiety in design, the off-white pale walls relieved a little by the deal pews and an immensely high pulpit, the highest I have ever seen. Second in importance to the pulpit, raised somewhat and placed beneath the pulpit, was the Set Fawr, literally the Big Seat; and here sat the deacons, who shouted 'Amen' when moved to do so by the appealing, or warning, words of our minister, Mr Jenkins.

Our pew was near the Set Fawr; and I have often thought that if Mrs Pankhurst had preceded my mother into this world at a suitable interval, Mam would have been raised to the Set Fawr.

Just before entering the sacred building my mother would always whisper, 'Always walk on tiptoe in the House of God!' and I would do so; although it was quite a long way to our pew, a journey made under the fixed stares of those already seated, a concentrated attention I felt acutely until others coming in behind us were given their share. Once in the pew, it was my duty to move a footstool for my mother's feet. My own feet dangled in the air when I sat, thus placing much of my body's weight on my bottom, a posture only really supportable to a child for long when there are cushions to distribute the weight. It was all right for a little while; but the seat was hard: so that finally I would seek relief by sitting for an interval on one cheek of my bottom,

then on the other, with variation when I used both. My mother would admonish in a whisper, 'Don't fidget!' but I could not help it. It was a great relief to stand up when hymns were sung.

The great height of the pulpit forced me to bend back my neck if I looked at the preacher; and when my neck ached, I would lean forward and lean my neck on the back of the pew in front where Mrs and Miss Pugh worshipped. It is true that the junior Pugh occasionally offered me an acid drop; and it is equally true that more often the senior, perhaps not liking a boy breathing down her neck, gave me an acid look.

If I glanced up at the gallery where May Jones sat with her mother, May would give me a wink with her left eye. This would automatically produce a nod from me, which would bring a hard nudge in the ribs and a sharp 'Stop that!' from my mother if she caught me; but I was unable to control that nod: whenever May winked I always nodded without for a moment knowing why. The junior Pugh's acid drop and May Jones's wink suggest a faint glimmer of fun in Saron Chapel; but otherwise the atmosphere was deeply serious and grave. No one ever smiled in Saron Chapel.

Even as a small boy who accepted without question the faith of his mother, I could not understand why people did not smile in chapel. God, as I pictured Him, was indeed a serious figure, but as the Creator of a cheerful world He must know how to laugh. And if He could laugh, why shouldn't we, in His house? I reached the bold and highly secret decision that God must be laughing at us in Saron Chapel for being so serious.

Something of the odour of sanctity still enveloped Mam when we got home after chapel. Here we might find Eliza if she had not been with us; and then Mam would tell her about the *pregaith* [sermon].

Wil Jon Edwards, *From the Valley I Came* (1956)

Drawing of underground revival scene. J.M. Staniforth

PRAYERS UNDERGROUND

Seventy yards from the bottom of the shaft, in the stables, we came to the prayer meeting. One of the workmen was reading the 6th chapter of St. Matthew to about eighty comrades. He stood erect amongst the group, reading in a dim, fantastic light that danced with the swinging lamps and vanished softly into the surrounding darkness. A number of lamps were attached to a heavy post closely wedged to support the roof, and around the impressive figure the colliers grouped themselves. Some were in the characteristic stooping posture, others half-reclined against the side of the road, with their lamps fastened to their pockets; others, again, stood in the middle of the passage. Earnest men, all of them; faces that bore the scars of the underground toiler; downcast eyes that seemed to be 'the homes of silent prayer'; strong frames that quivered with a new emotion.

Western Mail, 1 December 1904

Evan Roberts and the Revivalists from Loughor, postcard, c. 1905

MANNERS AT DINNER

Do not, when invited to dinner, arrive late. It is not fair on those who have invited you, nor their other guests.

Do not arrive late for dinner at home, for it causes conflict and bad feeling.

Do not sit a foot away from the table, nor right up against it.

Do not drink soup or broth from the end of the spoon. Do so from the side.

Do not make a noise when drinking, it is most unseemly. Do not ask for a second helping of soup.

Do not bend heavily above the plate; remain as straight as possible, without being stiff.

Do not break bread with your teeth; do so with your hands.

Do not eat with the knife. Never place the knife in your mouth. Do not fill your fork as if you were loading a cart, with your knife; raise with the fork only what you can easily lift, and no more.

Almanac Caergybi, 1909 (trans.)

POOR PARISH

In the parish of Llangattwg, Monmouthshire, although having 500 inhabitants, there is no church, no chapel or Salvation Army. The only place where a religious service can be held is The Rising Sun – the only tavern in the village.

Almanac y Miloedd, 1896 (trans.)

CROWDS HEAR MR EVAN ROBERTS AT MERTHYR VALE

To-night Mr Evan Roberts concluded his visit to Merthyr Vale, and all day long the services have been attended by crowds so great that it has been at times almost impossible to breathe.

The wonderful things about this movement are its spontaneity and its complete lack of organisation. I have not seen a single printed bill or circular telling when or where Mr Evan Roberts and the singing ladies will appear. But day by day the crowds of strangers get greater. This afternoon a young gentleman was present who had been sent all the way from London by his father to see if the accounts of the Revival were not greatly exaggerated. Ministers, evangelists, and missionaries, from all over the country, are arriving to seek a share in the great spiritual awakening. Day by day the trains are choked with visitors from the neighbouring valleys. The result is that these little chapels are utterly inadequate. At Calfaria last night there were many faintings, and the air was so bad that only with the utmost difficulty could Mr Roberts carry on his work. Arrangements are made for him to go from chapel to chapel that all may see him; but this is easier said than done. To get either in or out becomes almost impossible, besides, on a bitterly cold night, to pass from a bath of perspiration into the open air at hourly intervals is extremely dangerous. Mr Roberts has been warned that he must not undergo such risks.

This morning at the Methodist Chapel the crowd was tremendous, and there was a meeting full of power and prayerfulness. Madam Kate Morgan Llewelyn and the two

Llanilar Sunday School, 1913.
Arthur Lewis

Misses Davies were with Mr Roberts, and their singing had the most thrilling effect. A feature of the meeting was the earnest pleading of a young lady for the conversion of the girls and women of the district. At other chapels, from an early hour in the morning, simultaneous meetings were held and were distinguished by all the passion and fervour characteristic of this Revival.

Nearly all the shops were closed, and hundreds of colliers attended. The anger of the manager of one of the collieries here has been exhibited by the loss of work occasioned by the revival, and he has threatened that those who stay away shall do without any work until after Christmas.

At Zion Baptist Chapel this afternoon there were scenes of excitement, and the crowds even climbed up and stood on the windows. Miss Annie Davies sung a hymn in Welsh about the Bible and greatly moved the people as she held out the great pulpit Bible as the source and spring of their knowledge and salvation. Finally she fell forward with the sacred Book clasped to her breast and burst into a passion of weeping. There have been perhaps a score of new concerts at Merthyr Vale, but so thoroughly has the revival done its work already that among those attending there are few who have not already professed conversion.

At the neighbouring village of Treharris alone there have been seven hundred converts before the arrival of Mr Roberts, and all over the valleys invariably figures of the kind are announced. Mr Roberts is somewhat at a loss in dealing with these meetings of new converts where hardly a single unbeliever appears; but he pressed the need for entire concentration and faithfulness to the pledge they have given.

'Welsh Revival', *Daily News*, 16 December 1904

A GROWING ARMY OF SALVATION

This is a new sect in Wales. It is natural to ask who are they, and from whence they came. By their fruits are they known, and their work forces the most narrow of spirit to recognise that they are good people. It appears that one of the fundamental principles of the Army is self-denial; they place every feeling of fear and shame, and every tendency towards comfort and self-satisfaction on the cross once and for all and they consecrate their efforts to finding and keeping that which has been lost. It is remarkable how much physical and spiritual labour is accomplished by the women who hold positions in the Army. They parade the streets for hours of an evening, and they conduct rather long public meetings afterwards; they sing, pray, speak, the latter with strength; after that they continue their efforts hand in hand with forty or fifty applicants for Salvation and kneel in front of the Bench. . . . Have there been any in our country for years who are so apostolic in their hard and self-denying labour? . . . They are almost the only people to be seen reading the Bible on the train or along the roads. . . .

They are a type of pioneer rather than a church. It is an Army to make assaults on the enemy and to win victory for the Gospel. . . . Their care of their converts is remarkable. . . . The occasion of their coming to Wales disgraces us about the [condition of] the land before. . . . Is it not a shame that there is work in Wales for a sect like the Salvation Army at all?

Baner ac Amserau Cymru, 30 May 1888 (trans.)

HAS GENERAL BOOTH GOT IT WRONG?

General Booth's municipal honour scraping tour has been neither very dignified nor very successful. There is something peculiarly offensive in the professed follower of the lowly CHRIST going from town to town in a motor car. . . .

We will not discuss the question whether a place like Aberystwyth needs a religious organisation like the Salvation Army. Our own opinion is that the organisation is not needed and that it bears very little good if any. It may gather a little money in the summer season, but that money is obtained by setting a very bad example which is a pity. . . . We do not object to the worldly wisdom which General Booth has always manifested and we heartily agree with his conception that religion is more a question of social elevation than of spiritual salvation. General Booth for anything we know may have outlived his humility and may be now aiming at converting the Salvation Army into a highly respectable denomination. Whatever happens to the Salvation Army somebody is sure to begin again to work at the bottom of the social ladder. Ever since General Booth began his great work there have been enormous changes in reference to the attitude of Government towards the masses of the people. Those changes of attitude are in no slight measure due to the work of the Salvation Army.

Cambrian News, 9 August 1907

SPORT MUST BE SECONDARY TO DUTY

PREACHING SERVICES – Bethlehem Welsh Congregational Church held its annual preaching services on Sunday and Monday, when Miss Rosina Davies, Treherbert, and the Rev. John Davies, Cadle, officiated. . . . The sacred edifice was crowded on each occasion, especially Sunday afternoon, when several persons were obliged to stand throughout the service in the lobby. On this afternoon, both the Rev. John Davies and Miss Rosina Davies delivered rousing sermons. Miss Davies preached on the first verse in the 137th Psalm, 'By the rivers of Babylon, there we sat down, yea, we wept when we remembered Zion'. The Israelites, she said were here beginning to appreciate the valuable privileges which they had lost since being expelled from Zion. They had been surrounded with every luxury, until they had become, really and truly, the spoilt children of God. . . . There was room for fear that the people of Wales – home of the religious revivals and singing festivals – were not appreciating the privileges they had long enjoyed. There was some strong predilection growing upon Welshmen in favour of the football field and other like places. Every human duty seemed subordinated to sport and play. She had nothing against football in itself, but intensely prayed that people would realise that sport was secondary to work and duty, rather than the be-all and end-all of life as it was taken by so many persons now-a-days.

Aberdare Leader, 27 September 1902

Cardiff Salvation Army Band, postcard, c. 1908

Royal Welsh Male Voice Choir, postcard, 1909

Aberystwyth Town Band in 1900. Arthur Lewis

THE RHYMNEY CHOIRS

. . . the musical efforts of individual soloists were dwarfed by the achievements of the Rhymney choirs. There were, sometimes simultaneously, three of these: the large mixed choir, the male voice choir, and the ladies choir. Each of them won at the National Eisteddfod, the large choir five times, three times in succession. In 1911 it was invited to represent Wales at the Empire Festival at the Crystal Palace. Its conductor was a self-taught musician and a school attendance officer. The male voice choir conductor was a miner and the ladies choir was led by a young woman who ran a bakehouse. The rank and file produced their own leaders and obeyed them. The last rehearsal before the choir set out on its journey next morning to the contest at the National Eisteddfod was always a thrilling experience, often more musically impressive than the final rendering in the pavilion, where the rivalry and the repetition of the test pieces introduced disturbing elements. At home, in one of the larger chapels, the men in black, the women in white, row upon row rising to the rafters of the gallery, every eye riveted on the conductor, the men erect, the women more eager, bending slightly forward, all voices blending perfectly, all faces rapt in ecstasy, the singers were wafted away to a heaven of pure delight far away from the furnaces and coalpits.

This wide diffusion of choral singing and the frequent rehearsals throughout the winter provided a delightful recreation for many hundreds of men and women despite the rivalries and jealousies between choir and choir which marred the harmony. Every member was not only a performer but a musical critic. There can have been few homes in which snatches from the great oratorios and the set test pieces were not familiar. Handel, Haydn, Mendelssohn, and Joseph Parry, once a Dowlais puddler, were the popular composers. Bach and Beethoven were for the majority still in the future waiting to be introduced by Sir Walford Davies. From the male voice party we were always hearing the 'Destruction of Gaza', 'Martyrs of Arena', 'Italian Salad', 'Tyrol', and 'War Horse'. This last by David Jenkins of Aberystwyth was based on a famous passage in the Book of Job where the war horse 'smelleth the battle afar off'.

Thomas Jones, *Rhymney Memories* (1938)

AN AUDIENCE OF 20,000 JUDGES

About two o'clock I started out for the National Eisteddfod – showers of rain and hot sunshine chased themselves across Swansea – wondering whether there would be one. When I came within sight of the tent I saw that it was up, and I asked a policeman who stood near by, – 'Brother, is there anyone in that tent?' 'Anyone!' he answered, 'yes, there are twenty thousand people in it, and there are thousands more at the entrance who wish to go in.' I shall never forget the sight I saw. The enormous tent was overflowing, with neither floor nor bench in sight, only a restless sea of open-mouthed faces,

The Harry Collins Merry Mascot Minstrels in 1905. Arthur Lewis

– mouths clamouring for those on the stage to withdraw, so that the great Caernarfon choir might take its place. I understood that we were about to see the major choral competition. It was very difficult for the Caernarfon choir to begin singing, it was difficult to clear the stage . . . the crowd's patience was terribly short – in other parts of the tent an occasional argument turned into a fight; I saw a number of stick fights in the back benches, and the blows all fell on the hats of those who had neither part nor share in the argument. Things were getting worse, much worse, the audience boiling over, and Mabon [William Abraham] had to stand to look at them with as much hope of quietening them as if he looked over the boiling waves of the sea. Then, with the full strength of his voice he begins singing 'Land of My Fathers'. All dissension halted, all unworthy amusement quietened, the tumult abated, – and here were twenty thousand voices in glorious unison singing one of the tunes which, despite its meanness, is one of the national Welsh airs. . . .

. . . the male voice choir competition was about to begin, in front of twenty thousand judges besides the five musicians on the stage.

The Brynaman choir began – a workers' choir, enunciating excellently, but with rather harsh voices. After them came the Carmarthen choir – a choir composed of people with a more noble look to them, town shopkeepers and the sons of the neighbourhood's farmers. There was fire in their rendition of the 'Destruction of Gaza', but they lost a great deal of power by singing the 'Pilgrim' in English. Despite that they had charmed the audience, and the masses in the rear were drunk on music. The next choir was rather slow in coming up and the crowd diverted itself by giving the pitch, and their 'Doh' could be heard for miles. Before long the crowd themselves began singing, and we were given a rendition of 'Land of My Fathers' by a choir of twenty thousand. But now the Treorci choir was ready; men with the mark of labour on their faces. While listening to them the audience was as quiet as the grave . . . the crowd was in a blissful spirit by now, and when the choir finished the twenty thousand sang 'Huddersfield' with Emlyn Jones leading them. . . .

Railway poster advertising the Royal National Eisteddfod, 1906

Mr Rees Jones; Resolven, Mr T. Glyndwr Richards; Cynon, Mr W.J. Evans; Snowdonia, Mr John Williams; the London Welsh, Mr Merlin Morgan.

An excellent rendition of the piece was given by the different male voice choirs, but the Aberdare Male Voice Choir, that is the United Cynon, the best of all, and when the adjudication was announced the conductor received an enthusiastic and warm reception. Mr W.J. Evans is the son of Mr Rees Evans, who has been the famous conductor of the Aberdare united choir for many years, and we are pleased to note that Mr W.J. Evans has been recognised for some years now as one of the principal conductors of the Welsh Independents' Singing Festivals [Cymanfaoedd Canu].

He intends to return home tonight (Wednesday), and it is the intention of the townspeople to pay him his due respect. He will arrive at Aberdare by the 7.33 train of the G.W.R., and he will be met by the Party and town's Silver Band. A procession will be formed to accompany him to Aberdare Market Hall where a welcoming meeting will be held, and we trust that Aberdare traders will extend wholehearted support to the conductor and the party by displaying their flags to give them quite a welcome to them on their victory.

The party numbered about 120 in the competition, and we believe that considerable credit is due Mr W.J. Harries, Moss House, for his efforts in making the party comfortable in the Capital. He arranged places for them to lodge in the York, Waterloo and Savage Hotels, and corresponded with Mr D.A. Thomas who was so kind as to extend an invitation to luncheon at his own cost to the party in the three hotels, and sat at table with them in the York.

At the end of the luncheon the party paid a visit to Parliament (both houses) under the leadership of D.A. Thomas and Keir Hardie, the MPs for Merthyr and Aberdare, and Tom Richards, the MP for Monmouth.

Tarian y Gweithiwr, 2 March 1905 (trans.)

ENGLISH VERSUS WELSH

The triumph of Mr Harry Evans, FRCO, and the Dowlais Philharmonic Male Voice Society at the National Eisteddfod, Liverpool, 1900, saved Wales from extinction at the hands of their Saxon rivals and from the reproach of failing that year to score a choral success in the great Cymric festival. . . . The matter of expense had, unquestionably, something to do with the indifference manifested in South Wales. . . . Welsh choral singing had been greatly overpraised and lauded to the skies by their own countrymen and adjudicators, and, as a consequence, they had been led to believe that it was pre-eminently supreme. Hence no effort to improve it had been made, but they had simply moved in the same old grooves, and real progress was hampered. The standard of Welsh singing. . . . was not right; there was too much enthusiasm and too little technique and attention to detail. Besides, they were at a great disadvantage compared with the English choirs owing to the lack of good 'readers' of music and musical organisations, not merely choirs got up simply for competition or to perform a

Silence spread among the huge crowd then when the unvanquished Pontycymmer choir was seen to be ready. They were coalminers, and I find it difficult to believe that there are better singers in the world. The five judges were as though they had forgotten themselves, they had turned to the choir with faces wreathed in smiles of pleasure. 'Grand, passionate, inspiring' said the foreigner Signor Randegger of this singing. It is easy to believe that there were tears in Dr Parry's eyes in the hour of his triumph.

O.M. Edwards, *Tro trwy'r Gogledd. Tro i'r De* (1907) (trans.)

WELSH CHOIRS' ALBERT HALL TRIUMPH

Last Thursday, the annual Eisteddfod of the London Welsh was held in the Albert Hall. . . .

The major choral competition was 'Homeward Bound' by D.C. Williams. The choirs sang in the following order:— Manchester, Mr W.S. Nesbett, conductor; mid-Rhondda,

Sir John Williams with the foundation stone of the National Library of Wales, 1911. Arthur Lewis

work, and then, perhaps, to drop out of existence. . . . The case was not hopeless for their choirs usually possessed the better voices, had a more musical temperament, and, with the conductors giving more attention to technique the cultivation of a pure tone, there was no reason why the tide should not be turned in their favour once more.

'Choral Singing in Wales', *Western Mail*, 12 June 1902

A NEW NATIONAL LIBRARY

As the King remarked in his gracious speech, the National Library is to be 'a striking monument of national enterprise', and, when completed, 'will achieve the aim of its originators in that it will not only represent the language, literature and art of Wales, but will reflect every phase of the national life and industries'. The King and Queen and the acclaimed Prince of the people were there, fresh from scenes that had aroused feelings of deepest emotion and loyal devotion in the breast of the nation. They had brought with them all the concomitants of a Royal progress; and the Home Fleet was there, completing a scheme of the widest significance. It was not a local faction. Wales was there as a united Principality, and all the forces of national advancement in literature and art gloried in the event.

There is a romantic setting to these Welsh movements, and it is this stance of purposeful determination, on the part of the sons of the soil as well as of the privileged classes, to unite in an unbroken effort to better equip the rising generation in its march into Time that charms the stranger and rescues the Celtic race from the aspersion that they are a fitful, indeterminate people. The King has set his foot upon the detractors of the race. The year 1911 will mark the beginning of a period of rapid strides in national development.

'King and Queen at Aberystwyth', *Western Mail*, 17 July 1911

WOMEN'S TEMPERANCE

On Thursday, 22nd September 1892, under the presidency of Miss Gee, Denbigh, a conference of women, 36 in number, met at Bronwydd, Blaenau Ffestiniog, to consider the question of establishing Women's Temperance Societies in North Wales, with the aim of uniting societies already in existence, and to establish new ones, in order to disseminate the principles of Temperance and Purity. The aim was warmly approved, and all representatives undertook to establish branches in their different neighbourhoods. . . . As there was an unanimous feeling that the work would be fortified by general co-operation, it was decided that a Union of all the societies should be established called 'The Women's Temperance Union of North Wales'.

Y Gymraes, November 1896 (trans.)

Good Templars (temperance movement). T.T. Mathias

SAFEGUARDING AGAINST DRINK

When progressing from the child's world to that of the young man, a new chapter in his history opens, so that there is a danger that as his world changes he will alter his habits and put temperance to one side. So efforts should be made to organise some means for safeguarding his temperance in this dangerous period when he turns his back on the Band of Hope and he bids farewell to his home for the first time, facing the big wide world with its steep slopes and its many and varied temptations. How can this be done?

Union of Welsh Independents, Blaenau Ffestiniog, 1906 (trans.)

REFUSE DRINKERS ADMITTANCE TO CHURCH

We believe that the churches who refuse membership to inn-keepers are correct. Now, if it is right to do that, it is right to do the same with drinkers. We maintain that if selling drink renders a man unsuitable for membership, then buying it should do the same.

Union of Welsh Independents, Tredegar, 1905 (trans.)

PULLING PINTS ON PAY DAY

There was over eighteen pumps in the big bar alone and there was a small bar that men in working clothes weren't allowed in. On a Friday pay day, we'd have 23 people serving behind the bar, and when the hooter went for the men to come up we'd start drawing the pints of beer and put them under the counter. . . . There was a lot of drunkenness and nearly every Saturday night a lot of fighting. . . . Women were only allowed in the 'Jug and Bottle' . . . only about half a dozen women came in altogether to drink.

Bryn Lewis, Tonypandy

WEAKNESS IN THE CHAPEL

The weak and worthless whimperers of the pulpit, banded together, and supported each other with the confirmation of numbers. Their sense of shame was diminished by partition, and their seductive words deceived the multitudes. . . . In six months after the sacrilege, a statement of the case was given in the county association. Four of the rebels were present. One barefacedly denied the statement *in toto*, and lyingly alleged that the lease of the old chapel did not allow Temperance to be taught there. . . . The incorrigible chairman – a composition of nicotine and alcohol – had been to me for years, an object of scorn and pity. He had no want but his pipe and bottle. The stone Asbestos was not more unquenchable than his thirst. At the sound of decanters, he would fall into an ecstasy, as if he had heard the blast of golden trumpets, and tasted the joys of Paradise.

The Devil's Keys, Ystalyfera, 1888

Griffiths' Temperance Hotel, Tenby. Francis Frith & Co.

A famous fire and brimstone preacher, the Revd John Williams of Brynsiencyn captivating a congregation

Mount Zion Sunday (Cardigan?) School treat, 1897. T.T. Mathias

Chapter 6

ENTERTAINMENT

ow should the people use their leisure time? This question consumed the passions of commentators in press and pulpit during these years more than at any other time before or since. Even small reductions in the number of hours worked meant that leisure time became a much more important aspect of life for the majority of working people in the towns. Numerous activities — cultural, religious and sporting — all jostled for their attention and loyalties. From church and chapel to public house and music hall, from choral singing and cinema to spectator sports and gambling, new patterns of spending leisure emerged.

Mass spectator sports rapidly became a rooted aspect of life in the late nineteenth century, much to the dismay of many Nonconformist ministers who initially condemned such frivolous pastimes as a squandering of valuable time which might otherwise be better used for the glorification of God. The churches and chapels were also acutely aware that they faced a formidable competitor.

Of all sports, rugby came to embody Welsh national identity most completely. The game had been introduced into the country through the public schools but it was embraced with enthusiasm by working men, giving it a popular appeal which failed to develop in England, Scotland or Ireland. The Welsh Rugby Union was established in 1881 to enable Wales to compete on the international stage, and from the 1890s the Welsh team began to hold its own against other

rugby nations. During the first decade of the new century Welsh teams asserted their supremacy, winning six Triple Crowns between 1900 and 1911. Of all the achievements of this first 'golden era' of the Welsh game, it is the match against the previously unbeaten touring New Zealand side at Cardiff in 1905 which imbued the game with greater significance than that invested in the sport hitherto. It was from this date that rugby's unassailable position as the Welsh sport was established. Players of the period became household names.

Other sports flourished also. Soccer was not as popular as rugby but in the years before 1914 it had a stronger presence all over Wales than is often thought. Boxing emerged from the shadows of semi-legality to acquire a place at the centre of male associational life, prizing the macho qualities of strength and aggression while celebrating the fighter's skill. Freddie Welsh (1886–1927), born at Pontypridd, was the first winner of the Lonsdale Belt in 1909, five years later becoming the lightweight champion of the world. 'Peerless' Jim Driscoll (1880–1925), born in Cardiff of Irish parents, was another winner of a Lonsdale Belt who became featherweight champion of the world in 1909.

Visits to the seaside became popular with all classes of people, from Sunday School day-trippers to genteel ladies and gentlemen seeking to improve their health, while the peaks and crags of Snowdonia attracted members of the more adventurous leisured classes.

A day at the seaside, possibly a Sunday School outing. T.T. Mathias

Walkers reach the summit of Snowdon. Francis Frith & Co.

SNOWDON

Snowdonia, with its beautiful mountains and sequestered vales, is visited every year by thousands, and it is the aim of the hardy tourist to ascend the graceful and majestic king of hills, Y Wyddfa (the conspicuous one). Snowdon, by which it is more generally known, is a generic term for the whole range. . . .

Of the three best ascents of this mountain, the Llanberis route is very easy, and can be made on ponies the whole way.

By Capel Curig, courage and skilful climbing is required; and by Beddgelert – less adventurous than the latter, and more picturesque than the former – the ascent is fairly within the powers of an ordinary pedestrian.

We took the last-named route, travelling the first four miles in the Pont-Rhyd-ddu coach, and were deposited – alpenstocks, wraps and luncheon-basket – on the high road near a huge rock called Pitt's Head, from a supposed resemblance to the celebrated statesman. A guide was awaiting us, for being only ladies we had been prudent. He slung our impedimenta over his shoulders, and we started on our trudge; the 'brigand' – as we dubbed our guide from his picturesque costume of blue linsey and a Tam-c'-shanter cap – entertaining us with stories of a seafaring life. The sun was very hot, and we were glad of the shelter of some rocks, while one of the party sketched Llyn Cwellyn, which lay like a shield of embossed silver in the vale below, the gorse and heather on Castell Cidwm (Wolf's Castle) in bold relief. The path was rough from loose stones and very fatiguing, but at last we reached 'the ridge', about which we had heard a great deal, and we were glad to keep close to the 'brigand' while crossing it. The path is broad, and blocks of stone guard the edge, and it can only be really dangerous in a very high wind or thick mist; but the scene is grand, and very awe-inspiring, for immense hollows lie on either side. It is said that a stone dropped right and left over the edge, would be half a mile apart when they touched the bottom. The 'ridge' safely crossed, the topmost peak was disclosed, and against the skyline a string of ponies coming up with tourists from Llanberis, and shortly our four miles' climb was ended, and we stood on the summit.

Hot, breathless, and fatigued, we scarcely noted our surroundings, but dived into the luncheon-basket, and also put on our cloaks, for the air was sharp and cold.

But the grandeur of the scene woke in us the profoundest wonder. The atmosphere was clear all round. Mountains, hills, and lakes, peaceful valleys, winding rivers, and green woods, repeating themselves over and over again, melting gradually into the hazy blue of distance. The nearer view was of steep, abrupt outliers of rock, which pierced the air in jagged cliffs, and of vast hollows, many of them filled with water. These tarns were strangely weird and impressive – sometimes gleaming in the sunlight like burnished mirrors; sometimes black and still, until a breath of air would change their surface into rippling wavy lines of silver, obliterating the clear reflections of the mountains. . . .

The narrow space at the top was crowded with tourists, some clustering round the cairn in the centre, others refreshing themselves in the two hideous-looking huts. Below, in the shelter of a rock, ponies were tethered, and the whole scene was very animated and very incongruous in this vast solitude.

E.A. Kilner, *Four Welsh Counties: Brecknock, Caernarvon, Merioneth and Pembroke, A Holiday Book* (London, 1891)

Donkey rides at the beach, possibly Tenby, c. 1910. D.C. Harries

Bathing machines at Tenby. Possibly by Francis Frith & Co.

'QUEEN OF WELSH WATERING PLACES'

When walking along the clean and well-appointed streets of the town of Llandudno, when strolling among the thousands of strangers along the excellent promenade, the visitor will not find it easy to absorb the fact that as late as 1840 there was nothing there but an insignificant village, inhabited by a few fishermen and miners, and two or three farmers on top of the Gogarth. The place which previously was insignificant and unknown is today a popular resort of the many, and has won for some time the name of 'Queen of Welsh Watering Places'. . . .

The first question, of course, which enters the visitor's head is – Who was the saint after which this parish is named? Is any information about him available? In order to shed a little light on this question, I shall attempt to lead the visitor, in a leisurely fashion, to the top of the Gogarth, to the old church of Saint Tudno. We shall begin at the top end of the Promenade where a large and convenient pavilion has been erected, turning to the right. After passing the Baths Hotel, we come within sight of the sea, and from this spot we get a good view of the handsome pier in front of us, running into the sea for a considerable distance. We are now by the toll-gate, the entrance to Marine Drive, a road which was made several years ago round about the Gogarth mountain. This road is one of Llandudno's major attractions, and thousands can be seen walking along it during the summer months. A more romantic road cannot be imagined. Above us is a large and steep rock with a threatening appearance; beneath us is the sea with the roar of its waves sounding constantly in our ears. After walking for about a mile and a half between the rock and the sea, the visitor will see that the height of the rock gradually lessens, and soon, instead of looking up at a threatening rock, he sees the uneven sides of the mountain, and an occasional sheep grazing on its grass. After walking a little further, we come to a small path which leads from the road to the mountain above us. The first thing to meet our eyes after climbing up the side of the mountain along this path, is the ancient church of Saint Tudno. . . .

If we had continued along Marine Drive for another mile and a half, instead of turning to the path which leads from it to the church of Saint Tudno, we would have come within view of the handsome Pen y Gogarth lighthouse. A path on the right leads from Marine Drive to the lighthouse, which was built in a romantic place immediately above the sea. After entering and taking a look at the lenses, we start again and turn back to the road, and after walking for about five minutes, we arrive at a small gate in the wall, to the right of us. Underneath us we see a large and steep slope, sheep paths crossing it hither and thither, and if we but observe closely we shall see a winding path leading down to the rocks above the sea. If the reader is brave enough to follow me, I shall lead him now along a small, narrow and dangerous path above the sea. The wild view to be seen from this path is enough to cause us to grip the rock with all our strength. . . .

J. Tudno Williams, 'Prydnawn ar Pen y Gogarth' ('An Afternoon on The Great Orme') *Cymru* (1892) (trans.)

CRAIGSIDE HYDROPATHIC ESTABLISHMENT LLANDUDNO

. . . A Doctor resides in the House, and is at hand to advise concerning Baths and treatment, and in any case of emergency. . . .

The Water Supply is practically inexhaustible, coming from the Dulyn and Melynllyn Lakes, 1,700 feet above sea level. Moreover, all the water consumed in the House is filtered through the Berkefeld Filter, than which no more efficient filter can be procured.

The Climate of Llandudno has proven by statistics extending over a great number of years to be equal in mildness to that of any place on the South Coast of England, and this combined with the comforts and attractions of the Hydro renders Craigside an ideal place for a Winter Home.

Winter Tariff from 7/– to 10/6 per person daily
Summer Tariff from 8/– to 12/– per person daily

ALL BATHS FREE EXCEPT SEAWEED

JOHN L. HUNT
PHARMACEUTICAL AND PHOTOGRAPHIC CHEMIST COLWYN BAY

. . . sole proprietor of the celebrated Sea Spray Bouquet perfume [6*d* a bottle]

Dark-room for changing and developing Plates, Apparatus and Chemicals provided. The only Dark-room available to visitors in Colwyn Bay

BODNANT BOARDING ESTABLISHMENT AND PRIVATE HOTEL, LLANDUDNO

This Hotel is situated just off Church Walks at the foot of the Great Ormes Head. . . .
The Hotel is replete with all modern conveniences, the sanitary arrangements being perfect.
Accommodation for Cycles
DARK ROOMS FOR THE USE OF AMATEUR PHOTOGRAPHERS
Terms Moderate

Peeps at Picturesque Wales, 1893

Entertainment for visitors at the Castle Grounds, Aberystwyth. Arthur Lewis

An early photograph of the Menai Suspension Bridge. At the turn of the century, passengers on overcrowded motor buses often had to leave the bus, walk across the bridge and then climb aboard again for the remainder of the journey.

'VIBRATING MASS OF STUPENDOUS IRON-WORK'

. . . its appearance combines the solid grandeur of the Romans, who built for eternity, with the airy lightness of our modern chain architecture; and as we continue to gaze

Humorous postcard view of the Menai Suspension Bridge

from below, on this wondrous roadway suspended in mid-air, and measure the height of the banks, the width of the Strait, the comparative scale of surrounding objects, and the diminutive appearance of passengers among the gigantic chain-work, the tall vessels dropping down the river far beneath its level, our conceptions of the work, of its boldness of design, and skill, and labour of its execution, grow greater with every successive examination. Nor is it possible to cross it without experiencing a feeling of awe and of exultation, as it were, at so wonderful a result of human skill and energy, as from the vibrating mass of stupendous iron-work, to suspend which would seem, but for our familiarity with the process, to exceed the limits of mortal power. . . .

Description of the Menai Suspension Bridge from *The Tourist in Wales*, n.d.

A STARTLING COSTUME

We land now at the new pier, with its attendant crowds of fashionable idlers, among whom the tourist will probably see for the first time many wearers of the peaked Tyrolese hat, so common throughout Wales; a costume rather startling at first view, but when well worn, by no means unbecoming, with its adjuncts of a broad white frill worn upon the side of the face, a neck-handkerchief neatly adjusted, petticoats somewhat short and coquettish, dark stockings, and high shoes. The physiognomy of the people is also rather peculiar, being sharper and more acute, their hair and complexion darker, than is the case with the rounder and more massive 'Sassenach'.

Description of landing by boat at Beaumaris Pier from *The Tourist in Wales*, n.d.

AMONG GREAT CAMBRIAN MOUNTAINS

The pilgrimages of which I write are not made to Switzerland; my theme is a homelier and more humble one. . . . For small and simple as are these Cambrian hills of ours, when compared with the exceeding grandeur and vast complexities of the Swiss Alps or the Pyrenees, they are nevertheless gifted with essential features of true mountains – with ridge and precipice, cloud and mist, wind and storm, rain and torrent; nor are snow and ice wanting to complete the picture in winter-time. . . .

It is commonly said that the approach to Snowdon begins at Capel Curig; but this is a very short-sighted and unimaginative way of regarding so rich an experience as a pilgrimage to the heart of Wales. To the true mountain lover, the approach begins at Euston Square. Yes, there, in the great busy station when you have uttered the magic word, 'Bettws-y-Coed', and have received what looks like a mere railway ticket, but is, in fact, a passport to the enchanted fastnesses of the hills. . . .

Great mountains are all around you, but there is a sense of space and freedom, with wild slopes of grass and rock stretching up and back to the higher ridges that lie behind. . . . The sense of severity and aloofness which haunts these mountains . . . is due chiefly no doubt to their sterner physical features, and to the greater depth and bleakness of the bare valleys which intersect them, each group of peaks rising apart, like a mountain system of its own; but we Saxon visitors are also moved, perhaps, by a feeling of racial strangeness in a land which has no interpreter for us. . . . For me at least the first impression of 'angry grandeur' in the Welsh mountains has never been wholly obliterated by the intimacy of years, and has lent an unfailing zest to my walks. . . .

The character of the Glyder itself is that of a wild stony desert, upbreaking here and there, as notably at its summit, into bristling 'horns' and 'pikes' – stacks and shafts of rock piled together in fantastic disarray – wonderful in all weathers. But it is to Tryfan, even more than to the Glyder Fychan, that the heart of the pilgrim is drawn – that huge rocky bastion which juts out from the battlement of the main ridge . . . but so formidable is the look of the

A typical tourist postcard, stereotyping the Welsh dame and the English spoken by the natives

mountain that until about twenty years ago it was ascended by only one route, nor even now, when it has lost its former terrors, has it lost one jot of its impressiveness. After visiting Tryfan some dozen of times, I still feel its attraction as strongly as when I first discovered it, and I have sometimes thought that a summer might be well spent in making a thorough study of the peak, until one became familiar with the many unexplored recesses which the climber passes by, that labyrinth of cyclopean masonry – terraces and galleries, slabs and spires, turrets and gargoyles – with which it uprears itself, like the great cathedral that it is, to the two standing stones which form its crest. . . .

When we turn from the Glyders and Tryfan, still in their primitive state of utter wilderness, to their great neighbour, Snowdon, scarred and maimed by copper-mine and steam-engine, the change is a striking one; it is like passing from a perfect preserved work of art to some broken monument, the torso of a giant form, in which we have to reconstruct, from the beauty of what remains, the once exceeding splendour of the whole. . . . But crippled as Snowdon is, we may still find on it one incomparable excursion, the circuit of the great hollow of Cwm Dyli by the ridges of Lliwedd and Crib Goch, which, if we can shut our eyes to the abominations of slag-heap and railroad that must be passed on the way, will hold its own, even against the Glyder and Tryfan, as the grandest mountain walk in Wales. . . . Arrive *there*, what a scene awaits us, especially if the train has just steamed in with its latest freight of trippers! For consider on what ground it is that we stand – the very summit of the sacred hill, the shrine of Snowdon, once the pride and stronghold of the Cymry [the Welsh] . . . the natural sovereignty of Snowdon stands confessed; so truly imperial is its form, and so symmetrical do its superb ridges radiate from the parent peak.

H.S. Salt, *On Cambrian and Cumbria Hills* (1908)

Coronation Day at Aberystwyth. Arthur Lewis

Genteel outing to Marloes. D.C. Harries

A SUCCESSFUL SEASON

Many were led to believe that the merry-making of the Coronation and the Investiture would prevent strangers from visiting the bathing spots. During July there was some basis for this belief, because of the few visitors in our midst. But at the beginning of this month thousands of strangers came here, and they continue to come still. From Aberystwyth to Barmouth, and onwards as far as Pwllheli and Nefyn there are thousands of strangers now staying. Cricieth confectioners were so busy last week that they could not supply refreshments for the 80 Canadians who visited the town on Thursday. The local committee in charge of arrangements had to ask Miss Flower, of the George Hotel, to supply them with food, and this she did in the best manner. They paid a visit to the Llechwedd Quarry earlier in the day, and the interior parts of the quarry were shown to them by Mr R.M. Greaves, Captain Drage, and Mr William Owen, and they were also shown how to make slates. Afterwards they were given a snack in the quarry by Mr Greaves. They greatly enjoyed their descent to Minffordd in the 'little train'. They marvelled at the skilfulness of the designer of the railway and the engines.

Yr Udgorn (Pwllheli), 16 August 1911 (trans.)

'BUFFALO BILL'S WILD WEST SHOW'

The event of the season is close upon us – Buffalo Bill is within hailing distance and will arrive, with his great Wild West exhibition on July 4th.

There are not, in any other organisation for popular entertainment, so many hundreds of male performers and horses as appear in the arena of the Wild West, and not in many more 'shows' however pretentious they may be, are there such a number of men engaged in re-enacting for the

Playing hoop. D.C. Harries

public, thrilling incidents of real life in which they themselves have participated. Genuineness of personality in personation has been a distinguishing characteristic of this entertainment, ever since its first organisation by Col. W.F. Cody (Buffalo Bill). While the arenic performance is full of vivid, stirring Wild Western scenes, it has been expanded to take in a vast deal more illustrative of strong men and their doughty deeds all over the world and includes some splendid spectacular effects in the reproduction of the 'Battle of San Juan Hill', the most famous incident in the late Spanish-American war.

Aberdare Leader, 4 July 1903

BOXING MATCH ABANDONED

On Saturday evening a boxing match for a purse of gold took place at Mr J. Stokes's Pavilion, Market-place, Aberdare. The combatants were George Jones (Punch), Aberaman, and Con Sheen, Merthyr. When the fourth round was in progress a catastrophe occurred which brought the contest to a somewhat abrupt termination. The marquee suddenly collapsed and some of the spectators were so irritated by the course of events that they challenged the proprietor of the pavilion, and a lively altercation between them superseded the abortive boxing contest, which the referee declared to be a draw.

Aberdare Leader, 23 August 1902

Seaman with child, mid-Wales. Arthur Lewis

Llandeilo rugby football second team. D.C. Harries

WALES VERSUS NEW ZEALAND

I have heard of a crowd being too large to count. I saw it today in Cardiff, the capital city of Wales, and I have no desire to see its like ever again. A vivacious crowd composed of every nation under heaven, black and white and yellow – the true Welsh countryman, the self-confident Englishman, the black-skinned negro and the yellow-skinned Jap and Chinese, all congregated to watch thirty strong lads playing football. The boys of the Old Country had given England, Scotland and Ireland a beating, and today here they were facing, in a match which will live in history, fifteen of New Zealand's splendid players, players who are praised in every country under the sun. They swept away the English . . . they gave the Scots a beating they will never forget; and the staunch Irish were also prostrate under the powerful attack of these giants. And today Wales's turn had come – to be overcome or to achieve higher praise than has ever been their lot in the world of football. Little Wales! Here she is standing upright, without fear or trembling, like little David the shepherd, ready to send Goliath to the ground. And indeed, watching all the nations of the world congregated like this for the match, and hundreds and thousands of them basing their

hopes on the Welsh players, vociferously stating their sincere faith that Wales is worthy of the honour, the warm hearts of the Welsh in their midst cannot but leap with patriotic joy.

I understand an eisteddfod and a singing festival and a fair, but a business like this is beyond my comprehension. This is not the world of the mind; this, I think is a great eisteddfod of flesh, blood and muscles. An eisteddfod of the mind pulls thousands; but this attracts millions. Who said that the [Religious] Revival had killed the craze for football? There is little sign of that today, but let us admit that this immeasurable crowd is as intelligent, as respectable in clothing, as seemly in complexion as any which has ever been seen on a pitch. I did not hear an unseemly word and I did not see a sign of drink during the two hours we were at the field. But here are the players on the pitch, and the shouts of welcome tear through the air. . . . The contest is about to begin. The visitors are dressed in black; and the Welshmen are in red jerseys, with the Prince of Wales white feather on every chest.

How many people are present? Fifty thousand, it is said. Now every throat is extended, every mouth open, and every voice hoarse with loud words of encouragement for the staunch Welshmen. 'Play up, Wales', is the cry, and an enthusiasm like electricity lights up the entire enormous crowd. It is seething and raring to go.

It has begun! Wales take the first kick, and the ball is like an arrow in the air heading towards the goal. The Welsh are like gluttons after it; but in an instance the strangers meet with them, and the battle is intense. Back and fore, up and down the pitch the competitors run. The New Zealanders are big and robust, powerful in every sinew, but the Welsh beat them in speed and skill, and against expectations the Welsh players prevent the New Zealanders from getting their own way in the scrum. There our boys do a little more than hold their ground. Indeed, for the first twenty minutes the Welsh if anything get the better of the contest. It is they who attack and the strangers defend. The New Zealand goal is often in danger, and the contest is equal. The crowd moves back and fore like a forest in a hurricane in its anxiety. Hooray! Wales have crossed the line. The first try is on the board, the hero being Teddy Morgan of London. The conversion attempt is a failure. But, what joy! Who can describe the scene? Fifty thousand mortals have lost their heads in a wave of ecstasy. And this is the first time, it is said, that the New Zealanders have yielded since they arrived in this country. Listen to the happy shouts. Wales has won! What the other nations of these islands have failed to achieve, has been done by the race of old Britons. . . . The clamour is deafening. This is a night like the unforgettable night of Mafeking. Ring the bells! Throw up your hats! Wave the flags! Wales is victorious! Her success is celebrated throughout the world! Hooray! Hooray! H-O-O-R-A-Y!!

Gwilym Hughes, *South Wales Daily News*, 18 December 1905 (trans.)

THE ART OF RUGBY FOOTBALL

Football is the historic national game of England. It is, in its primitive forms, the essence of nearly every form of modern sport. Today there is no game to equal it, both in the popular and the scientific phases. The game demands not only trained and sound physique, but the well-balanced mind, sane judgement, tact and resource. Its finest exponents may well represent a nation mentally active and physically strong. So far we have not been on debatable ground, but we must come to less firm ground. The New Zealanders came to this country with a great reputation and it has been more than justified. On Saturday morning the leading London organs of public opinion had no hesitation in saying that as a body of athletes these visitors were unequalled, and to be overcome by Wales, the smallest of all nationalities was an 'unthinkable contingency'. We return to unassailable facts. Nothing had interfered with the triumphal march of Colonials. Before them England, Scotland and Ireland went down. They had come to be regarded as invincible, Wales was the last of the nations to be met, and the coming contest was regarded as the greatest of the century. Feeling ran high from Land's End to John o'Groat's. Excitement was intense. Public enthusiasm was as fervent as on the morning of some great Waterloo when the destinies of Empires hung in the balance. Cardiff for the

day was centre of interest in the Old and New World. Never before in the history of the greatest of all games was there such a situation. Would Wales prove equal or superior to the great victors? Or would she fail as the rest had failed? That was the situation on Saturday morning. All the world knows what happened in the afternoon. Wales broke the spell; she accomplished what the sister nations had found impossible, she achieved the highest record in the annals of modern sport. When you consider for a moment what Wales had to do, and when you think of how she did it, there arises in every man the feeling of highest admiration for qualities that find the most popular expression. The men – these heroes of many victories – that represented Wales embody the best manhood of the race. And here we are met with some of the greatest problems in the development of distinct nationalities. We all know the racial qualities that made Wales supreme on Saturday: but how have they been obtained? Wales has more restricted choice of champions than the other nations. She has had fewer opportunities in the exercise of some of the mental and physical powers than the nations with ancient Universities and wider fields of training. It is admitted she is the most poetic of nations. It is amazing that in the greatest of all popular pastimes she should be equally distinguished. The

'Victory!' Even the great Welsh scalp hunter has himself lost his hair – the great win for Wales in rugby football against Ireland at Cardiff by six tries to nil. J.M. Staniforth, 1903

A boxing boy in the studio of D.C. Harries, Llandeilo

Proving that even in south Wales, football was played! D.C. Harries

well-known orator and writer who lectures in the Park Hall, Cardiff to-night has elaborated the theory that the great quality of defence and attack in the Welsh race is to be traced to the training of the early period when powerful enemies drove them to their mountain fortress. There was developed, then, those traits of character that find fruition today. 'Gallant little Wales' has produced sons of strong determination, invincible stamina, resolute, mentally keen, physically sound. It needs no imaginative power to perceive that the qualities that conquered on Saturday have found another expression in the history of Welsh education: that long struggle against odds that has given the Principality her great schools and her progressive colleges. The national traits are equally apparent in both contexts.

South Wales Daily News, 18 December 1905

A BOXING MATCH

It is no exaggeration to state that nothing short of an international Rugby football match could have stirred gallant little Wales like that great boxing match between Jim Driscoll and Freddie Welsh. At half-past seven, when the preliminary contests that are the hors d'oeuvres, the great hall was a wonderful sight. It was a vast sea of expectant faces from wall to wall. It reminded me of the multitude that night at Olympia when Hackenschmidt broke Madrali's arm after a minute's actual wrestling. Probably in the whole history of boxing in this country no such crowd has ever been got together for a glove contest. The atmosphere was subdued, but one felt the electric undercurrent that was to be set free later on by the appearance of the champions. The waiting movements were beguiled by a band which played national

Llandovery School Girls Hockey Team. D.C. Harries

tunes; but, whereas Rugby crowds amuse themselves in similar circumstances by bursting into song, there was no vocalism last night, and for once even the familiar 'Land of My Fathers' failed to inspire the musical soul of the Principality. . . .

Suddenly Welsh was being driven back, across, and round the ring, with Driscoll butting his chin. There could be only one end to this, and Mr Bettinson, springing between the men, awarded the fight to Welsh, on an unmistakable foul. The next instant, Driscoll having thrown a passionate gesture with his gloved hand at Welsh, cheers reigned supreme. Two of the rival seconds began to have a mild set-to with the knuckles, and the ring was crammed with spectators. Driscoll was half-dragged to his dressing-room, almost crying with temper. But he had brought his fate on himself. So far as it had gone, Welsh had been the better boxer, but the nasty spirit of the contest will leave unpleasant memories for those who saw it.

Morning Leader, December 1910

WORLD CHAMPION

The great fight is over, and a Welshman this morning wears the crown of light-weight champion of the world. Freddy Welsh, of Pontypridd, at the end of twenty rounds with Willie Ritchie of San Francisco, at the Olympia, London, last evening, was declared to be the winner on points. . . .

Gymnasts, Carmarthenshire. D.C. Harries

Salmon fishing on the River Towy. D.C. Harries

Merry-go-round, St Margaret Fair, Tenby, 1913

Many years have elapsed since a boxing contest of such world-wide importance was last seen in London. . . . As might be imagined, Americans in London rallied round their man, and turned up in great force to see him uphold the boxing honour of his country, while large crowds of Welshmen were seen around the ring.

So great was the interest aroused in America itself that special cables were laid on right into the building so that the reports of the match might be transmitted direct to New York, whence of course they were flashed across that great continent to San Francisco . . . while close at home the *South Wales Daily News* were in direct touch with the ring and by a telephoned round by round description were letting Welsh's compatriots know how their favourite was progressing in the great fight of his life. Altogether it was a great night in the history of boxing in this century.

Welsh prepared himself for the contest at Porthcawl, on the south coast of Wales, where his tremendous energy had astonished all those who were assisting him. . . .

In addition to the title the men were meeting for substantial money, Ritchie being guaranteed £3,000 and Welsh 50 per cent, of the ratings after the expenses and Ritchie's share had been deducted. . . .

About a quarter to nine the hall was filled up nicely. . . . Ladies again patronised the proceedings, and if the bookings were to be taken as a guide, fully 2,000 of the fair sex were expected. Society was strongly represented, and the number of spectators in evening dress, both ladies and gentlemen, was quite remarkable, the costumes of some of the ladies forming a bright patch of colour in the otherwise sombre aspect of row after row of people. . . .

At length, a minute or two before 10 o'clock, Welsh entered the ring, and a loud cheer went up as he was seen approaching. . . . Then, amid silence, a large number of his fellow-countrymen began to sing 'Land of My Fathers', the notes of the thrilling melody soaring up into the roof of the huge building in most inspiring fashion. Welsh immediately stood up, and smiles came over his face as he

Landau carrying tourists to Conwy Castle

looked towards the quarter from where the tune came, and slightly bowed his acknowledgements. Welsh, who looked in excellent fettle, was attired in a rich silk gown of quiet shade.

Five minutes elapsed, and then up went another roar as Ritchie, attired in a dark red and violet dressing gown, entered the ring. . . . So at a quarter past ten the great combat began. . . . And so the round went until the finish of a contest which left Welsh a ridiculous easy winner on points. Directly the round had ended, and before the men could get to their corners, the ring was stormed by a crowd of people who carried Welsh to his corner, and then a terrific shout went up when it was realised that at last Welsh had won for the United Kingdom the light-weight championship of the world.

It was a great victory, attained by wonderful all-round skill, speed, and ability. There was never any doubt, after the first six rounds, as to what the result would be, and the referee had no need to announce who had won.

South Wales Daily News, 8 July 1914

Picturesque abbey ruins at Tintern

THE CHAMPION CYCLIST'S FUNERAL

I remember one evening when Twm and Dai came home from the pit earlier than usual. . . . There was one occasion when they had a legitimate reason for coming out early. They wanted to attend the funeral of Arthur Lynton, the champion cyclist of the world in his day. There had been a good deal of talk about this funeral which, in its way, had international significance; and my curiosity had been excited to such an extent that I became far from sure whether I, so young and small, was worthy to attend the funeral of so distinguished a man. I thought it wisest not to leave the question for my mother to decide.

I recall the event most vividly. It was the largest funeral I have ever seen, stretching for two miles with thousands of people lining the route from the town to the cemetery. Apart from local people, the mourners seemed to have come from every country in Europe. Many of the wreathes were designed in the form of cycles; but perhaps the most impressive sight, apart from the actual wreath-decked coffin, was a Frenchman (I knew he was a Frenchman because he wore a beard) riding a bicycle immediately behind the coffin, the form of the bicycle being cleverly outlined in flowers. Being too young and small, I was jostled here and there until I found myself more or less settled in a prominent position immediately behind a brass band playing a solemn tune which I have since identified as the 'Dead March in Saul'. I was blissfully unaware that a fairly large hole in the seat of my pants permitted a good deal of shirt to emerge, but in the sombre glory of the occasion perhaps this was not noticed as much as my mother evidently feared it had been with consequent disgrace to the family. . . .

People talked of this funeral and the famous people who attended it for weeks after. I heard Twm tell Dai that he had seen no less a person than Jimmy Michael; and Dai told Twm that he had seen Tom Lynton, the late champion's brother. Both became world champions later.

And I remember hearing our lodger, Harry John, telling a highly interested group of people how Arthur (the late champion) had trained on Haulier's Tip before going forth into the world to beat all rivals and to become its champion.

W.J. Edwards, *From the Valley I Came* (1956)

Tourists arriving by donkey at Oystermouth Castle, c. 1900. D.C. Harries

An early travelling cinematograph at Pwllheli at the turn of the century

BUYING A CAMERA

My dear Elin,

I am going to begin amusing myself, instead of working myself to death. And the way I am going to amuse myself is by learning how to make pictures; not by doing the work slowly, with a brush and pencil . . . but by removing the cap from the lens of a camera, and in an instant a picture is taken. I am going to buy a camera, it will cost only twenty pounds, and go some day to J.M. Jones to learn. . . .

Ever faithful, Owen.

Owen M. Edwards to Ellen Edwards, 20 March 1891 (trans.)

THE INFLUENCE OF FICTION ON THE MINDS OF THE YOUNG

At Swansea Quarter Sessions on Friday last 'penny horribles' and bioscope pictures of burglaries were said to have influenced two youths in committing a number of burglaries and stealing jewellery. Their names were Pendarvis Tagholm and David John Harris and they at once pleaded guilty. For the prosecution it was stated that the prisoners appeared to have entered on a career of crime after reading sensational fiction, their favourite work being *The Life of Charles Peace*. Detective Sergeant Howard said that the boys had seen bioscope pictures of a burglary and they stole a revolver and dagger to arm themselves like the hero of the pictures. The Recorder in binding the prisoners over under the Probationers Act said that if they went into a music-hall or any place of that kind or entered a public-house within the next two years they would be brought up and sentenced.

The Bioscope, 9 October 1908

PASSENGER TRAINS

The desire of the inhabitants of the Colliery district round Pontypridd to come to the Barry Sands found expression in a deputation from the Pontypridd Local Board and other bodies asking that passenger trains should be run to Pontypridd and the Rhondda. Although the Company had applied for these powers, the opposition of the Barry and Cadoxton Local Board had caused the rejection of the measure. The Company had also endeavoured to get a better connection with the Rhondda Valley for passenger traffic: Parliament refused to sanction a line from Hafod to Porth.

Leave was obtained to extend the railway from Barry to Barry Island for the purpose of developing Barry Island as a seaside resort. Early in 1895, the Contract for making the railway was let to Messrs. Price and Wills, and the railway was opened for public traffic in August 1896. Powers were obtained in 1896 to extend the Island Railway to the Low Water Landing Stage, and this extension was opened for traffic in 1897.

History of the Barry Railway Company, 1884–1921

Picturesque fishing smacks, Tenby. Francis Frith & Co.

Seaside attractions at Borth, a small holiday village on Cardigan Bay. The village would be brimming over with visitors from the Midlands during the summer months. Arthur Lewis

Chapter 7

POLITICS

From the 1880s down to 1914 the Liberal Party enjoyed an almost total domination of political life in Wales. At no point during these years did the Conservatives come within realistic striking distance of loosening the Liberals' grip on the allegiance of the people, a fact demonstrated in startling fashion in 1906 when the Tories failed to carry a single constituency in the principality. Whereas Liberalism had become identified with the national aspirations of the Welsh people, the Conservative Party was perceived as being English, alien and wedded to the interests of a small, privileged minority.

Religion, education and national identity were the major issues animating Welsh political life during these years. Top of the Liberals' wish-list was disestablishment of the Church of England in Wales, a demand which formed the coping-stone of the Liberal programme until the measure was finally passed in 1919. Unlike the Irish, Welsh nationalists displayed little enthusiasm for Home Rule. This was made crystal clear by the failure of the 'Cymru Fydd' (Young Wales) movement during the 1880s and 1890s. The Liberal leader William Gladstone had succeeded in tapping into the circumscribed sense of nationality by praising the Welsh and visiting the country frequently; he had a home at Hawarden in north-east Wales and his personal connections with the country helped cement his enormous popularity.

For much of the period up to 1914 the Liberals succeeded in winning and retaining the support of working men, large numbers of whom had received the vote in 1884. William Abraham ('Mabon'), a prominent Rhondda trade union leader epitomised this success: he was a Liberal MP who preached the gospel of conciliation in union affairs and moderation in politics. This viewpoint still predominated at the turn of the century. However, there were stirrings of a new kind of labour politics with the establishment of the Independent Labour Party in 1893 and the Labour Party itself in 1900. Keir Hardie, a Scot, was elected as Wales's first socialist MP at Merthyr Tydfil in 1900. During the following fourteen years Liberal strength in industrial south Wales would slowly but surely crumble in the face of Labour's onslaught, as class attitudes in the region polarised and the Liberals' organisation atrophied.

Another shot across the bows of the Liberal consensus in the decade before the First World War came from the women's suffrage movement. 'Votes for Women' was the cry of a relatively small number of activists, although many more women than those who joined one of the women's suffrage societies and took part in their processions and protests undoubtedly sympathised with the aim. In 1912 some suffragettes, including Margaret Haigh, later Viscountess Rhondda, took direct action to further their cause. By 1914 the Liberal Party was beleaguered in the south Wales coalfield, but it tenaciously clung to its grip on Welsh politics until after the war.

Suffragette disturbance at Llanystumdwy

Cartoon by J.M. Staniforth

LIBERALS AND THE FIGHT FOR RIGHTS

Why is Wales so overwhelmingly Liberal at the present moment? It is not to instal one statesman in office. It is not to deprive one party of power in order to put another in power. It has been done because Wales, by an overwhelming majority, has demonstrated its determination to secure its own progress. Wales has returned the men most in sympathy with its need – to fight for its rights.

David Lloyd George, speech at Conwy in 1892

GIVE THE PEOPLE THEIR DUE

I examine every political subject in its connection and its influence first on my own country and after that on Ireland. . . . Wales has suffered, and is suffering, from oppression and bad laws. Welsh endowments and Welsh public posts, and the control of Welsh matters are still not in the hands of the body of the population. Landowners take the fruit of the toil of the farmers and the labourers, and as in Ffestiniog and other places they claim ownership of houses built by the workers. The control of the drink trade and rates and the administration of justice is in the hands of magistrates who are out of sympathy with the majority of the Welsh nation. Whether in Parliament or outside Parliament I am determined to do my part energetically and tirelessly to undo these injustices.

Thomas Edward Ellis, MP for Merioneth, 1897 (trans.)

A TRUE NATION

The present decade is witnessing a remarkable revival of national sentiment in Wales. In every direction there are unmistakable signs of a true *renaissance*. Our prestige as a nation was never so high, and the recognition of our national individuality never so marked and thorough. In proof of this

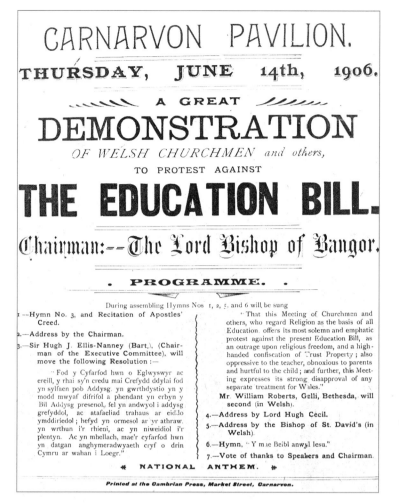

Poster proclaiming a demonstration against the Education Bill, 1906

we may refer to that full enjoyment which is now ours of educational advantages which have long been denied our country. The language of our hearths is no longer branded with the stigma of the Education Department but on the contrary has received due homage by its introduction into the Code. The connecting link between elementary and higher education is now being established while the national colleges are in the hey-day of prosperity. Then, in addition to this, we may cite the establishment, by Royal Charter, of the new University, as a tribute to the distinct nationality of Wales, no less than a symbol for a people's passion for knowledge. Further evidence of a fuller recognition of our national individuality may be addressed from the present attitude of the Imperial Parliament in reference to Welsh questions. Never before were the claims of the Principality to legislation, conceived in full sympathy with the national sentiment of its people, so strongly emphasised. In the appointment of the Land Commission – invested with full powers to inquire into the strained and unhappy relations that have so long existed between the landed gentry and the industrious peasantry of Wales – and in the foremost place now given in the programme of the Government to Welsh Disestablishment, the true seer will not be slow to discern the coming of the day spring for the nation's hopes and desires. Everything points to the advent of the Welsh people to a large and a fuller life. Our claim to a national individuality is no longer ignored or disputed, but, on the contrary, it is agreed that whatever goes to the making of a nation, be it history, race, language or soil, the Welsh people are fully entitled to the status and dignity of a true nation.

Moreover, indications are not wanting that the Welsh nation is conscious of the glorious possibilities that now lie in its path. The artificial divisions, which have so long been fraught with bane and detriment to our welfare as a people, are being swept aside; and the landmarks of sectarianism are rapidly disappearing. A growing sense of unity pervades all sections. The centripetal forces are already at work. Men are being drawn together by the magnetic force of patriotism, and by a keen desire that Wales should take its place among the nations and realise, to the fullest extent, its appointed mission for the benefit of mankind. But what, it may be asked, are the methods that should be adopted in order to attain such an end? The consideration of such a question as this has resulted in that latest development of national activity – the Cymru Fydd [Young Wales] movement. It is the pervading consciousness of the inadequacy of old methods, under the stress of present-day needs, and of the urgent necessity of a readjustment of national aims and ideals that has given birth to this new spirit of Nationalism.

J. Hugh Edwards (ed.), *Young Wales*, Vol. 1, January 1895

DISESTABLISHMENT BEGINS

Mr H.H. Asquith, on rising to ask for leave to bring in the Welsh Suspensory Bill, was received with loud Ministerial cheers. He said: In moving for leave to introduce a Bill to prevent for a limited time the creation of new interests in the Welsh Church I am undoubtedly asking the House [of Commons] to take a first step towards the Disestablishment and Disendowment of that Church. (Cheers.) . . . the policy of Welsh Disestablishment is a policy to which the Liberal party is on the whole distinctly pledged. . . . What is the position of the Church in Wales? For generations past it monopolised the whole Parliamentary representation of the country. It has owned in days gone by – I don't mean as a body, but through its adherents, the landlord class – almost the whole of the land in Wales. Until a time which is in the memory of almost the youngest of us, Churchmen have filled the magistracy and all the offices of public trust. It dominated for generations the Government and the teaching of the Grammar schools, and it controlled the charities and the endowments of the country. The Church therefore had at her disposal, and behind her throughout this controversy, of which we are now approaching the close – (hear, hear) – every material force in the country.

South Wales Daily News, 24 February 1894

MEETING ON SNOWDON'S SLOPES

A meeting which was looked forward to with profound interest took place on Tuesday afternoon at Cwmllan, the slope of Snowdon, at a point which is some 1,200 feet above the sea and

W.E. Gladstone addressing a meeting at Cwmllan on 16 October 1892

about equidistant from Beddgelert and Rhyd-ddu, if a cross mountain path be taken from the latter village. The gathering was in every way unique and beyond doubt unprecedented. . . . To this remote and inaccessible place about fifteen hundred people journeyed from Carnarvon and all the adjoining districts, a large number of them being leading men in the Liberal ranks. The special ceremony for which the gathering was convened was the dedication to the public for ever of a new road which Sir Edward Watkin had constructed from Cwmllan to the top of Snowdon. A platform had been erected partly on a rock and partly on an improvised dry wall, and was carpeted and fitted with chains. In addition to Mr and Mrs Gladstone . . . Mr W.J. Williams, the well-known musical conductor, of Carnarvon, led the audience in singing several Welsh hymn tunes, the effect, as may naturally be supposed, being very remarkable. The first was the furious 'Bryn Calfaria', and with the rendering of this the meeting was virtually opened. . . .

After some more singing had been enjoyed, Mr Gladstone, who was received with loud cheers, said: I am sorry the hymn has come to an end (laughter). I was delighted to hear it, and I wish it had gone on (cheers). I should have been much better employed in listening to it than I can possibly be in saying any words to you, and it is not in my power to give such satisfaction by anything I may say as you have given to me by the pleasure of listening once more to your national Welsh music, sung in the national Welsh style – (cheers). . . .

If the Welsh had more differences of opinion among themselves it would be much easier to speak upon them – (laughter), – but the Welsh all say pretty nearly the same thing – (renewed laughter). You have given us of that very great and good evidence in sending us 28 members out of 30 to speak the same thing in Parliament – (Hear, hear), – I should not be at all surprised if upon some other occasion not only the 28 but the 30 Welsh members were all to sing in unison. . . .

The Premier spoke for some fifteen minutes and upon his resuming his seat Mr W.J. Williams again addressed to the front of the platform, and under his conductorship the crowd gathered below sang with great power, 'Bydd myrdd o ryfeddodau' and 'Duw mawr y rhyfeddodau maith'.

North Wales Observer and Express, 16 September 1892

THE EPITOME OF THE WELSH MP

. . . the embodiment in which we have clothed our political views for a House of Commons representative. He is the very inclusion of every quality of personality, experience and

A pro-disestablishment meeting

Gathering rushes. The poster declares a meeting to oppose the Welsh Suspensory Bill. D.C. Harries

capacity which has made for an ideal Welsh representative. This Welsh mining area is Labour in every aspiration but, since man cannot live by bread alone, the Rhondda mining electors are Nationalists, they are Nonconformists to an overwhelming degree, and the whole gamut of social reforms come within their ambition for a better Wales and a better living condition for the masses.

Rhondda Leader, on William Abraham MP 'Mabon', 1910.

LABOUR NOT SOCIALISM

Those who have read my previous articles in *Y Geninen* know that I said nothing disrespectful about the Labour movement in this country, nor about its leaders. I was careful to distinguish clearly and definitely between 'Labour' and 'Socialism'. A man can display his sympathy with the rights of Labour without embracing the Socialist system. I shall go further: without possessing the slightest . . . of sympathy with Socialism, and without believing for a second the windy assertions of the party's leaders, I retain the right and the ability to defend the legal rights of the workers and to argue their case at all times.

Revd W.F. Phillips, *Y Ddraig Goch ynte'r Faner Goch?* [The Red Dragon or the Red Flag?] (1913)

THE RED DRAGON AND THE RED FLAG

. . . Liberalism is willing to improve the lot of the working-man, but still leaves him a working man, a hireling belonging to a subordinate and disinherited class, and that is exactly what the worker has determined not to be. (Cheers.)

Our movement is no parochial one. In every country under the sun to which production for profit has found its way, there is to be found a great and constantly-growing Socialist movement. On its banners is inscribed 'Peace on earth and good will among men'. We hear much in these days of Welsh Nationalism. Most of it is poor, spurious imitation of the genuine article. I have no use for that kind of Nationalism which indulges in high-sounding phrases on the platform, but is silent when striking Welshmen are being shot down by English soldiers. (Cheers.) The characteristics of a race can never die; but whatever differences of race there may be, we are first and foremost human beings. That is the message of Democracy to a world weary of fret and strife and pillage and murder, however these may be glorified by high sounding titles. Have the Red Dragon of Wales by all means as your national symbol, but have it blazoned on the Red Flag of International Socialism. (Loud cheers.)

Keir Hardie, *The Red Dragon and the Red Flag* (1912)

Cardiff Suffrage Pilgrimage to London, 1908

ALL SOUTHERN WALES COMES TO SWANSEA

Swansea has been the scene for many a demonstration in the cause of progress and of freedom, but never was she the centre of such a marvellous outburst of popular determination for securing the last concession needed for the realisation of complete equality in religion as that which we recovered to-day. 'We give them numbers' was the national response to the challenge of the bishops, who, fighting still for civil as well as religious authority over Wales, dared as a last resource to make pretence in England that the people of the Principality are lukewarm in support and insincere in their demand for Disestablishment of the alien Church within their midst.

Lukewarm! Then why this multitude? They came from every town and village in the southern and most populous half of Wales, from the mountain side in hundreds, from remote towns and villages in thousands, from teeming valleys of industrial activity and commercial towns in tens of thousands. They came from every centre, all inspired with one all-absorbing determination: the levelling of barriers which divide religious people and which too long have made

it possible to maintain amongst a freedom-loving population a state Religion for the few.

All of Southern Wales was there, not, perhaps, in body, but still there none the less. They were there by direct representation and by delegation. Every progressive body throughout the vast expanse of hill and vale, hamlet and busy town was represented by its own contingent, specially accredited for the purpose. And so the tens of thousands who flowed into Swansea from morn till noon represented not alone themselves, but hundreds of thousands more.

And they were represented in another way as well. Every member of the Welsh Progressive members of the Senate was there in heart and spirit; all but three or four, whom illness and pressing calls prevented, were present in the flesh to voice a mandate given at the hustings election after election for nearly fifty years that Wales shall have her freedom from the shackles of an alien institution. And then, above all, was present for the first time in Wales's history the outward visible indication that the Government of this great and mighty Empire is with the movement heart and soul. Else why the presence on the platform of the three personages occupying high positions in the Government. . . . Never before has Wales had such recognition in a Government – when four of her representatives have been raised to high official rank. Never before on a political platform, in Southern Wales at least, has one seen so many members of Government united in the realisation of a great national movement.

All roads led to Swansea yesterday. The day was the eve of the crowning triumph of the people, and realising the importance of so great an occasion people vied with one another in the honour of participating. They came from north and south and east and west. No less than fifty-five trains were specially chartered, and quite as many ordinary trains aided in the influx of visitors. Even these proved insufficient. And so the railway companies had to duplicate them by the dozen. And yet so great was the demand that at station after station people had to be left behind.

South Wales Daily News, 29 May 1912

THE STATESMAN AND THE SUFFRAGETTES

Llanystumdwy, the little village on the shores of Cardigan Bay where the Chancellor of the Exchequer spent his boyhood, is already an established shrine with many pilgrims. It has authentic relics. To-day as many pilgrims as could manage to squeeze themselves in took tea in the little cottage which used to house young Lloyd George and his uncle, and many others shyly plucked keepsakes from its ivy-mantle front. Few could make the complete round, for the narrow arteries which served the village were soon choked almost to bursting point. . . . All these things were duly admired and commentated on by the hero-worshipper, who usually observed that this secluded valley between the mountains and the sea was the very place which he had pictured as the cradle of a statesman who had brought new imagination into British politics.

The festival was marred by a revolting woman hunt, in which four poor deluded but astonishingly brave women were left to the promiscuous violence of a fiercely excited crowd. It had begun with every promise of success. The day was perfect for an outside gathering, and 7,000 or 8,000 people had come from all parts of North Wales to do honour to a man whom Wales idolises. The occasion was the ceremonial opening of the Institute and Club which the Chancellor, with a mind to the deficiencies of the village in his boyhood days, has presented to Llanystumdwy. . . .

Everything went as merrily as a wedding-bell until the chancellor himself the only Cabinet Minister present, rose to address the audience. . . . With insensate folly, four women . . . interrupted in turn. Mr Lloyd George had not finished his pacific appeal before a woman near the barrier which separated the crowd from the privileged seats gave a hysteric

shriek. It was only 'Votes for Women', and in an open-air meeting of this size its effect as an interruption was negligible. But the crowd had sharp ears, and the crowd, which had been singing 'Land of our fathers' with religious fervour a few minutes before, now burst into fury. Fortunately for the victim she was within a short distance of the outskirts and her passage to the house of refuge to which the police at last conducted her was easier than that of her sisters. I could not follow her progress sufficiently to speak from the personal observation, but there is ample evidence to show that she was struck repeatedly on the way. Mr Lloyd George was obviously distressed, and renewed his appeal that future offenders should be let go scatheless. 'Turn them out, if you like,' he cried, 'but don't do them any harm. They are misguided; they are inflicting damage on their own cause which it will take years to repair.' 'Nonsense,' shouted a woman in the middle of the crowd. She had grey hair, but that was no protection. The bystanders struck at her with fists and sticks, and she was in danger of being trampled underfoot when two burly policemen came to her rescue. . . . Mr Lloyd George shook his fists in passionate denunciation of the acts of violence on the part of people in the throng. 'Bring her to the platform,' he shouted. But the field slopes towards the platform, and in the rush downwards the woman was badly mauled. The women who were sitting in the reserved seats took fright, and crowded over the press table on the platform. The Chancellor jumped on to the table and tried to quieten the crowd by starting 'Land of our fathers'. The majority, sober-minded people . . . joined in, but a ruffianly remnant still pursued the chase, and only the valiant efforts of the policemen . . . saved their charge from ducking. . . . One poor girl had her jacket and blouse stripped from her back, and was carried into a neighbouring house in a state of collapse, with her face bleeding. . . . Altogether it was a disgraceful scene.

Manchester Guardian, 23 September 1912

GOVERNESS

I have seen no reference in the course of this correspondence to the pathetic case of the nursery governess. Why should she – who has perhaps seen better days, who is perhaps a lady (think of it!) – be dragged through the weekly ordeal of plastering nasty stamps on a grimy card? My blood boils when I think of the blush of shame mantling her humble brow, the more so as this duty will doubtless have to be performed in the presence of that vast army of prying, peering, callous, gossiping new officials which is growing every day – the minions of a radical government.

Westminster Gazette, 22 November 1911

Chapter 8

DAVID LLOYD GEORGE:
FROM COTTAGE-BRED BOY TO DOWNING STREET

For many people David Lloyd George (1863–1945) epitomised the core values of Welsh Liberalism and, indeed, of Welsh national identity at the turn of the century. His formidable oratorical skills and piercing invective were legendary, and few contemporaries could match him for the sheer power and controlled passion of his public speaking. During his long stint in government from 1906 to 1922 he would hold many of the major offices of state, becoming Chancellor of the Exchequer in 1908 and Prime Minister of an Empire at war in 1916. Yet Lloyd George was also one of the most controversial politicians of his generation. An 'outsider' in British terms, he took on the might of the House of Lords and won. He was also accused of selling honours for political gain, and the 'Welsh goat' incurred disapproval and condemnation for his extra-marital liaisons.

Born in Manchester in 1863, his widowed mother shortly returned to north Wales where the young David was heavily influenced by his Uncle Lloyd. Quick-witted and with a rebellious streak, he honed his oratorical skills as a solicitor in the courts and soon achieved notoriety as a young man who was no respecter of social status. He became known as a staunch defender of the rights of the Nonconformist people against the overbearing power of the established Church in a number of causes célèbres which gained him valuable publicity. As a result of this high profile activity he was chosen to contest the Carnarvon Boroughs by-election for the Liberals in 1891, winning the seat with a slim majority. He would represent the

seat until his retirement from Parliament shortly before his death in 1945. He would bestride the imperial stage when he became Prime Minister in 1916, finally losing power ignominiously in 1922.

In the 1890s Lloyd George championed the politics of Welsh Home Rule but when the prospect of success faded he concentrated his energies on climbing the greasy pole at Westminster. Following the Liberal landslide of 1906, he piloted path-breaking radical social legislation through the Commons, most notably concerning national insurance and pensions, in his 'People's Budget' of 1909. His actions provoked a row with the House of Lords which led to the famous 'Peers against the People' general election of December 1910, resulting in reform of the upper House which curbed its powers to frustrate the will of the elected Commons. Unsurprisingly, he was a favourite figure for political cartoonists.

Lloyd George has also been seen as something of an enigma, a man whose life was riddled with contradictions. While he may have built his political reputation as a gritty and eloquent champion of Welsh grievances against the power of the aristocracy and the Established Church, in 1911 he participated in the Investiture of the Prince of Wales at Caernarfon Castle with relish. That the event took place in his own constituency was a factor of some relevance. Similarly, at the end of his life the scourge of privilege finally made his peace with the Establishment by accepting a peerage, taking the title Earl Lloyd George of Dwyfor.

'Hallucination: Dame Wales (in the flesh): Well indeed now, by his talk he do fancy it wass me backing him up; but he is mighty mistaken – certainly not with them kind of gloves on, look you!' J.M. Staniforth

'At Port Arthur. Captian Morganoff: General, our ammunition is very low; shall we capitulate? General Lloyd-Georgiskoff: No; for goodness sake hold on a bit longer! We must reserve fire.' J.M. Staniforth

Lloyd George as Chancellor

HOUSES OF PARLIAMENT ARE DISAPPOINTING

Went to Houses of Parliament – very much disappointed with them. Grand buildings outside but inside they are crabbed, small and suffocating, especially House of Commons. I will not say but that I eyed the assembly in a spirit similar to that in which William the Conqueror eyed England on his visit to Edward the Confessor, the region of his future domain. Oh vanity.

Lloyd George, diary entry, Saturday 12 November 1880

SELF-GOVERNMENT FOR WALES

There is a momentous time coming. The dark continent of wrong is being explored and there is a missionary spirit abroad for its reclamation for the realm of right. That is why

I feel so sanguine were self-government granted to Wales she would be a model to the nationalities of the earth of a people who have driven oppression from their hillsides, and initiated the glorious reign of freedom, justice and truth.

Lloyd George, speech to the South Wales Liberal Federation, February 1890

THE MIGHTY SPIRIT

The spark of patriotism has been like the genii of the Arabian fable. It has burst asunder the prison doors, and given freedom to them that were oppressed. It has transformed the wilderness into a garden, and the hovel into a home. It has helped to drive away poverty and squalor, and brought riches and happiness in its train. It has raised the destitute into potentates, and bent monarchs to its will. Now this is the mighty spirit

A pro-Lloyd George cartoon postcard

which has wandered homeless and aimlessly amongst our hills. Let us requisition the powerful aid of a force which has done so much for our fellow men in other countries.

Lloyd George, Cardiff, 1894

THE TRUEST CELT

One of the main elements of Mr Lloyd George's character is push. He is largely endowed, too, with worldly wisdom. A superficial observer may pronounce him rash and indiscreet; all who are thoroughly familiar with his history will, however, unite in saying that his rashness and indiscretion must be more apparent than real, for they always prove advantageous to him as a party politician by strengthening his position in his constituency and in the country generally. . . .

Mr George has a very interesting personality. He is very affable, very frank and outspoken. He has a bright and intelligent face and (in private life) very pleasing manners. . . .

Take him for all in all, he seems by far the best-fitted of the Welsh members for the leadership of the National party in the House of Commons. . . . He is quick-witted; he is eloquent; he is daring; in a word, he is perhaps the truest Celt that Wales has ever sent into the House of Commons.

T. Marchant Williams, 'Mr David Lloyd George' in *The Welsh Members of Parliament* (1894)

A SLUMP IN DUKES

Industries which were making losses last year are beginning to make profits this year. . . . Only one stock has gone down badly – there has been a great slump in dukes. They used to stand rather high in the market, especially the Tory market, but the Tory press has just discovered that they are of no value. They have been making speeches lately. One especially expensive duke made a speech, and all the Tory press said 'Well now, really, is that the sort of thing we are spending £250,000 a year upon?' Because a fully-equipped duke costs as much to keep up as two *Dreadnoughts* – and they are just as great a terror – and they last longer. As long as they were content to be mere idols on their pedestals, preserving that stately silence which became their rank and their intelligence, all went well and the average British citizen looked up to them. . . . But then came the Budget. They stepped off their perch. They have been scolding like omnibus drivers purely because the Budget cart has knocked a little of the gilt off their old stage coach. Well, we cannot put them back again.

Lloyd George, the Palace Theatre, Newcastle, 9 October 1909

'500 MEN, CHOSEN ACCIDENTALLY'

Let them realise what they are doing. They are forcing a revolution, and they will get it. The Lords may decree a revolution, but the people will direct it. If they begin, issues will be raised that they little dream of. Questions will be asked which are now whispered in humble voices, and answers will be demanded then with authority. The question will be asked whether five hundred men, ordinary men chosen accidentally from among the ranks of the unemployed, should override the judgement – the deliberate judgement – of millions of people who are engaged in the industry which makes the wealth of the country.

That is one question. Another will be: Who ordained that a few should have the land of Britain as a perquisite? Who made ten thousand people owners of the soil, and the rest of us trespassers in the land of our birth? Who is it who is responsible for the scheme of things whereby one man is engaged through life in grinding labour to win a bare and precarious subsistence for himself, and when, at the end of his days, he claims at the hands of the community he served a poor pension of eight-pence a day, he can only get it through a revolution, and another man who does not toil receives every hour of the day, every hour of the night, whilst he slumbers, more than his poor neighbour receives in a whole year of toil? Where did the table of that law come from? Whose finger inscribed it? These are the questions that will be asked. The answers are charged with peril for the order of things the peers represent; but they are fraught with rare and refreshing fruit for the parched lips of the multitude who have been treading the dusty road along which the people have marched through the dark ages which are now emerging into the light.

Lloyd George, the Palace Theatre, Newcastle, 9 October 1909

ROUGH WEATHER REAPS ITS REWARDS

Yesterday I visited the old village where I was brought up. I wandered through the woods familiar to my boyhood. There I saw a child gathering sticks for firewood, and I thought of the hours which I spent in the same pleasant and profitable occupation, for I also have been something of a 'back-woodsman'. And there was one experience taught me then which is of some profit to me today. I learnt as a child that it was little use going into the woods after a period of calm and fine weather, for I generally returned empty-handed; but after a great storm I always came back with an armful. We are in for rough weather. We may even be in for a winter of storms which will rock the forest, break many a withered branch and leave many a rotten tree torn up by the roots. But when the

weather clears you may depend upon it that there will be something brought within the reach of the people that will give warmth and glow to their grey lives, something that will help to dispel the hunger, the despair, the oppression and the wrong which now chill so many of their hearths.

Lloyd George, the Pavilion, Caernarfon, 9 December 1909

GREAT LITTLE NATION

Ah! The world owes much to the little five-foot-five nations. The greatest art in the world was the work of little nations; the most enduring literature of England came when she was a nation the size of Belgium fighting a great Empire. The heroic deeds that thrill humanity through generations were the deeds of little nations fighting for their freedom. Yes, and the salvation of mankind came through a little nation. . . . Wales must continue doing her duty. I should like to see a Welsh Army in the field. I should like to see the race that faced the Normans for hundreds of years in a struggle for freedom, the race that helped to win Crecy, the race that fought for a generation under Glendower against the greatest captain in Europe – I should like to see that race give a good taste of its quality in this struggle in Europe; and they are going to do it.

Lloyd George, Queen's Hall, London, 19 September 1914

Postcard depicting the House of Lords 'throwing out' the famous Lloyd George budget

Chapter 9

POMP AND CIRCUMSTANCE

*A*s a consciousness of national identity developed and town life became more sophisticated, there emerged also a desire to cultivate more elaborate public ceremonies as symbols of material progress and civic pride. During the nineteenth century, public ceremonial mainly occurred on occasions such as the opening of new docks which served to underline the economic prowess of individual towns. In the years before the First World War, however, a new type of pageantry was developed which placed an emphasis on the national dimension to local celebrations. This was evident in the first 'village pageant' in England and Wales, held at Builth Wells in 1909. The two central events of these years were Cardiff's National Pageant of 1909 and the Investiture of the Prince of Wales at Caernarfon Castle in 1911.

A crucial factor in the success of a pageant is the splendour of the context within which it is held. Both Cardiff and Caernarfon offered great, if somewhat different, possibilities in this respect, especially as both boasted impressive castles. At Cardiff, the Third Marquis of Bute had used the fabulous wealth he had accumulated as a result of the growth of industry to restore the city's castle, and in 1909 it provided an imposing context for a pageant which drew heavily on the country's medieval history. When the event was finally staged, the crowds who came in their tens of thousands to witness the spectacle were treated to a

production composed of twenty-seven events crystallising the main developments in the fifteen centuries of Welsh history from the days of Caradog's battles against the Romans to the Act of Union with England in 1536. At the same time as celebrating the heroes of the past, it emphasised the loyalty of the Welsh to the present-day Empire.

Although sharing many of the features of the Cardiff National Pageant, the Investiture held in Caernarfon's medieval castle was a very different kettle of fish, in large part because this was the first time that an important royal ritual had been held anywhere outside London. There were no precedents, no existing guidelines as to how the event should be conducted. As there had never before been an investiture of this kind, the elaborate ceremonial and sumptuous costumes were invented for the occasion, even though the impression was given that this was a time-honoured ceremony stretching back centuries. Royalty was busy re-inventing itself as a popular institution at the turn of the century, and the Investiture of 1911 can be seen as one part of that larger process.

On the whole, the people expressed their support for the monarchy, and vociferous critics like Keir Hardie, the MP for Merthyr Tydfil, were few in number. Nevertheless, it was noted that enthusiasm for the Investiture was muted in the south Wales coalfield where industrial relations were bitter and riots had recently occurred.

'River Wye and Tributaries' at Builth Pageant, 1909. P.B. Abery

BUILTH WELLS PAGEANT 11 AUGUST 1909

Episode I

Characters: Father Time, River Wye and Tributaries

Scene 1: A Druid Teaching a Class

Scene 2: Archdruid Cutting Mistletoe

Scene 3: Chieftain Hirwallt bringing coward before the Archdruid.

Chorus: 'Land of Liberty and Light.' Air: 'Over the Stone'.

Episode II

Characters: Father Time, River Wye, Britons, Cyflym Tegwen, Maximus (a Roman General and Soldiers), Arch-Druid etc.

Scene: A British Village, men with coracles and strings of fish greeted by Villagers. Cyflym announces the coming of the Romans.

Chorus: 'Here around the Sacred Oak'. Air: 'Captain Morgan's March'.

Episode III

Characters: Father Time, River Wye, Elwedd (a chieftain with early Britons), Druid, and St Cewydd and Followers.

Scene: A British Village, Conversion of Elwedd to Christianity.

Chorus: 'Though night's sable folds, etc.' Air: 'Mai'r flwyddyn yn Marw'.

Episode IV

Characters: Father Time, River Wye, Idnerth and Jevan (two Welsh Chieftains), and Philip de Braose.

Scene: Philip de Braose (Lord of Builth) holds his Court, and deals out mock justice, and the consequent indignation of the Welsh.

Chorus: 'Hark! the trumpet's notes resounding'. Air: 'Hark afar the bugle sounding'.

Episode V

Characters: Father Time, River Wye, Prince Llewelyn, The Lord of Llechryd, Mortimer, and L'estrange.

Scene: The meeting of Prince Llewelyn and the Lord of Llechryd, who advises him not to proceed to Builth Castle. He proceeds, however, persued by L'estrange and Mortimer. Thirteen Fairies, draped in black, dance to a dirgis. The Monks of Abbey-Cwm-Hir return from Builth with the body of Llewelyn.

Chorus: 'Gwalia is striken'. Air: 'Marsh of Rhuddlan'.

Episode VI

Characters: Father Time, River Wye, Mr Gwynne of Llanelwedd Hall, and Parish Clerk.

A Bridal Scene

Revels, Pavane, Morris and Maypole Dances, etc.

Chorus: 'Hail! The happy marriage morn'. Air: 'On this day'.

Episode VII

Characters: Father Time, River Wye, A Quaker, First Player, and Tom.

Scene: A party engaged in a game of bowls – the Quakers admonish them, and exhort them to turn their thought to higher things. Huntsmen cross the scene with hounds.

Chorus: 'Buoyant hearts and laughing faces'. Air: 'Hunting the hare'.

Mr Arthur Price, 'The Court Jester' at the Builth Pageant, 1909. P.B. Abery

Episode VIII

Characters: Father Time, River Wye, Crier and Clerk.

Scene: The Old Disserth Forest.

Dances: Barn-Dance and 'Sir Roger', 'Mari Lwyd Lawen', Grinning through the Collar etc.

Chorus: 'Martial strains, etc.' Air: 'Springtime is now returning'. 'Hen Wlad fy Nhadau.' 'God save the King.'

❖ ❖ ❖

Builth Wells has excelled itself! Never before had the town and district risen into such prominence, and given the outside world anything like the 'treat' they had at the historic pageant. But it has meant untold labour and patience, and the magnificent success comes as compensation to all, and undoubted justice was done to its varied epochs by the leading characters. Almost forgotten customs were resurrected, and the fun, the celebrations, and rejoicings of ages agone were, for the hour, presented to the vast throng with such realism. Old things became in the truest sense, new; and the present generation realised, for once, that the fathers of by-gone centuries compressed something of interest and incident into their lives.

Brecon & Radnor Express, Thursday, 19 August 1909

Postcard advertising the Cardiff pageant; from a colour drawing by
J.M. Staniforth

UNITY

The glorious history of the Principality set forth as an object
lesson could not fail to instil into the minds of the young the
higher patriotism that in their forefathers kept Wales a distinct
national unity and made her a more powerful factor in
Imperial progress because she was true to herself.

South Wales Daily News, on the idea of a National Pageant,
22 September 1906

THE NATIONAL PAGEANT

During the last few years we have seen or heard about many and
admirable pageants whereat were reproduced in their proper
places the gayer or nobler scenes of local history which the
towns that presented the pageants had achieved or merited
distinction and fame. This National Pageant of Wales, however –
apart from being the greatest ever held in point of magnificence

and numerical strength – is the first function of its kind which is
fully and voluntarily representative of an entire nation.

Comparisons are odious; but it does not seem invidious to
point out in the premises that this is also the first pageant of
its kind wherein all classes of the community have lent their
services with such loyal patriotism.

Many of the stirring scenes it depicts were enacted under
the shadows of that same Cardiff Castle beside which the
pageant is being held to-day. In such circumstances perhaps it
is not so remarkable that the charming chatelaine of that
historic structure, the Marchioness of Bute, should accept for
the nonce the rôle of 'Dame Wales'.

When, however, we find the part of 'Owen Glyndwr'
being taken by the gallant veteran of Balaclava, Viscount
Tredegar; when we find the Mostyns in the North and the
Bassets of Beaupre on the South, Lady Llangattock on the
East, in Monmouth, Lady St. David's on the West, in
Pembroke, and nearly all the great historic county families
'betwixt and between', alike taking their own ancestors or
other characters in the various scenes of the pageant, we
realise that this is really a National Pageant of Wales. And not
only do such notable leaders of society assume the rôles of
great historical personages in this pageant, but by a happy
coincidence scarcely possible outside the pale of the
Principality, the parts they play are those of their own families'
ancestors. For example, we find Lord Mostyn of Mostyn Hall
impersonating the gallant Richard ap Howel of Mostyn, from
whom he is directly descended, and to whom Harry Tudor
presented his sword, when the Welsh chieftain refused all
other reward, on the bloody field of Bosworth, that was five
hundred years ago. A thousand years earlier, a still remoter
ancestor of the Mostyns lived in the person of Princess
Tregaingl, the grandmother of King Arthur the Great. The
head of that senior branch of that royal line to-day is Sir Pyers
Mostyn of Talacre. His daughter takes the part of Tregaingl,
and the younger Miss Mostyn takes that of Tregaingl's sister,
the Princess Gwen from whom she is also descended.

Then when we see half a thousand of the crack football
players of the Principality careering wildly across the field, as did
the wild tribesmen they represented what time they were led,
half naked, by Ivor Bach, and won Cardiff Castle from the mail-
clad Norman defenders – then do we recall the fact that, on the
mimic battle grounds of the national sport, Wales leads the three
kingdoms to-day, and that her youths are still as stout of heart
and strong of limbs as they were when they followed Harry of
Monmouth to Agincourt, and smote with British swords and
bows of British yew the flower of the chivalry of France.

Pageant of Wales, *Pictorial and Descriptive Souvenir Booklet*
(1909)

THE CAERNARFON INVESTITURE

Of all the great ceremonies that take place in the summer of
this memorable year none, surely, is of greater interest or
greater significance than the Investiture of His Royal
Highness the Prince of Wales in his Principality. It is a long

time since such a ceremony has been performed at all. It is still longer since it was performed in Wales. . . .

The main idea in forming the processions has been to associate the Prince of Wales as far as possible with the people of Wales. His procession will contain, therefore, the elected and similar officers and such persons as have some special national significance. It is to be headed by the Archdruid and the officers of the Gorsedd, and these will be followed by the Mayors of all the Welsh boroughs and the Welsh members of the House of Commons. In the King's procession, which follows, will be the high sheriffs, the lord-lieutenants of the counties, the peers, the ministers, and the great officers of the State. After the address and a gracious reply from the Prince there follows a religious service. This is unprecedented, but it was naturally felt that the ceremony would be incomplete without it. It will emphasise more than anything has done for many years the unity of the various Christian denominations in Wales, the service being jointly conducted by ministers of the various churches, and one of the most admirable features in connection with the investiture has been the absolute harmony in the preparation of this portion of the ceremony. Throughout, a choir will provide that music which is indispensable at any great gathering of Welsh people; but without doubt there will be something more impressive than the harmonious perfection of a trained choir; there will be the spontaneous burst of song from all the thousand present when the Prince is acclaimed. Nothing is more moving than the way in which any gathering of Welsh people sing 'Hen Wlad fy Nhadau' [Land of My Fathers] for no national anthem equals it in feelings and in beauty. At Caernarvon, on the occasion when for the first time in history Welshmen and Welshwomen of all estates and from all corners of the Principality are gathered to celebrate their loyalty to the great traditions of their past, and to assure the world of their determination to earn a yet more illustrious future, their united voices will be something never to be forgotten. Nobody questions the vitality of the Celtic people to-day; and Wales is proud of her position and her children. By acclaiming their Prince on July 13th the Welsh people will show once more that personal loyalty which has ever been one of their most marked characteristics. Welsh people possess the gift that is essential to loyalty and the gift of imaginative sympathy, and the heart of every Welshman will go out to the boy prince who comes amongst them.

W. Ormesby-Gore, 'The Investiture of the Prince of Wales', *Wales*, 1911

MILITARY INVASION

A brilliant and imposing sight was presented by the troops drafted into Caernarvon for the Investiture ceremony. Considerably over 12,000 in number, the vari-coloured uniform and head dresses of their respective units lent a colour to the proceedings which will not readily be forgotten. It was probably the largest and most striking military ceremony parade ever witnessed in the Principality. What made it all the more interesting was that the majority of the troops were drawn from Wales, the Territorial Force in particular being very largely represented.

The military invasion of the town had been going on for days past, amongst the earliest arrivals being the 2nd Battalion of the Welsh Regiment, who won warm appreciation for the expeditious manner in which they pitched the tents for the accommodation of the troops at the three large camps established at Coed Helen, Griffith's Crossing and Bethel Road. The thorough manner in which the arrangements were carried out reflected great credit upon Lieutenant-general Sir Henry Machinnon, K.C.B., C.V.O. of the Western Command, who was director general. Major-general Sir Francis Lloyd, K.C.B., C.V.O., D.S.O., as the head of the Welsh Territorial Division, was entrusted with the command of the troops lining the route of the Royal procession, and in this capacity he added to his already enviable reputation by the splendid use he made of the troops at his disposal.

'An Inspiring Military Spectacle', *Western Mail*, 14 July 1911

The Most Noble, the Marchioness of Bute, 'Dame Wales' at the Cardiff pageant, 1911. C Corn

Caernarfon investiture of the Prince of Wales, postcard, 1911

CROWNING GLORY

Now that the Royal tour in Wales has come to an end it is possible to look back calmly and critically and to form a true opinion as to its success. There is no doubt as to its success as a pageant – it was a magnificent triumphal progress such as has never been witnessed in Wales before, and, as Mr Balfour publicly remarked, the Investiture ceremony will always stand out in one's memory as one of the most brilliant functions of modern times. As a medium whereby the Welsh people could demonstrate their loyalty to the Throne and to their Prince, it served its purpose in an unparalleled degree, and the nation is grateful to their Majesties for the opportunity afforded. As a reflex of the Royal approval of Welsh national life and aspirations nothing could have been more inspiring, and the past week will at all times be re-called as the crowning time in the Welsh renaissance.

'King and Queen at Aberystwyth', *Western Mail*, 17 July 1911

AN APPETITE FOR CHANGE

In the coal-mining areas where the people are left alone by the aristocracy and the pomp of the palaces and the daily life of the aristocracy is unknown, the people are not so servile and subservient. Although there is not much democracy and next to nothing of opposition to the Crown, there is one thing that is growing and that is the unwillingness to accept things as they are. Socialism has never grown like it is now growing in the coalfield. While the North takes a holiday to worship the King and Prince, it is the things that tend directly to change the nature of society that are important in the South.

Llais Llafur, 22 July 1911

AN ENGLISH KING AND HIS ROBBER BARONS

Wales is to have an 'Investiture' as a reminder that an English King and his robber barons strove for ages to destroy the Welsh people, and finally succeeded in robbing them of their lands, driving them into the mountain fastnesses of this native land like hunted beasts, and then had his son 'invested in their midst'.

Keir Hardie, 1911

ACKNOWLEDGEMENTS

PHOTOGRAPHS

All the photographs reproduced in this volume are from the Photographic Collection of the National Library of Wales. The majority have been printed from their original negatives, and the authors would like to thank the staff, current and former, of the Reprographic Unit of the National Library, especially Mr Stuart Ladd and Mr Gareth Lloyd Hughes, for their painstaking work in producing the prints for this volume.

The authors also thank Mr William Troughton and Mr Lyn Lewis Davies of the Department of Pictures and Maps of the National Library for their assistance with the picture research for this volume; Mr Robert Davies and Mr Michael Francis for their assistance with additional graphic sources; and the staff of the Readers' Services of the Department of Pictures and Maps, the Department of Manuscripts and Records, and the Department of Printed Books of the National Library for their ready assistance.

Thanks are ultimately due to the photographers, their heirs and successors who ensured that these original photographic items were donated to the National Library of Wales. Without their foresight, the majority of these images, and thousands more besides, would have been lost from view forever.

TEXT

The authors wish to thank Ms Nia Williams for her assistance in the compilation of the text sources and Mr Huw Ceiriog Jones and Mrs Marian B. Hughes for casting a professional eye over the proofs.

The authors have made best efforts to trace and credit copyright holders of extracts reproduced in this compilation, and each known author and photographer is credited in the body of the text. Despite these efforts, it has not been possible to trace every copyright holder, and the authors wish to apologise for any omissions which may have been made.

In particular the authors wish to thank the following:

- The Rhys Davies Estate for permission to use extracts from *Print of a Hare's Foot* (Heinemann, 1969)

- ISIS, The Education Support and Inspection Service, for permission to use extracts from *The autobiography of Edmund Stonelake* (Mid Glamorgan County Council, 1981)

- Mrs M.M. Wheatley for permission to use extracts from *The History of Ebbw Vale*, by Arthur Gray-Jones (Ebbw Vale District Council, 1970)

Gathering for a wedding. Arthur Lewis

INDEX